ROLE PLAYS

A Sourcebook of

Activities for Trainers

DAVID TURNER

**KOGAN
PAGE**

First published in 1992

Apart from any fair dealing for the purposes of research or private study, or criticism or review, as permitted under the Copyright, Designs and Patents Act, 1988, this publication may only be reproduced, stored or transmitted, in any form or by any means, with the prior permission in writing of the publishers, or in the case of reprographic reproduction in accordance with the terms of licences issued by the Copyright Licensing Agency. Enquiries concerning reproduction outside those terms should be sent to the publishers at the undermentioned address:

Kogan Page Limited
120 Pentonville Road
London N1 9JN

© David Turner, 1992

British Library Cataloguing in Publication Data

A CIP record for this book is available from the British Library.

ISBN 0 7494 0765 4

Typeset by DP Photosetting, Aylesbury, Bucks
Printed and bound in Great Britain by
Biddles Ltd, Guildford and King's Lynn

Contents

Acknowledgements

I would like to express my thanks to a number of people who helped me while I was preparing this book. First is my wife, Poppy; without her the book would not have been written. In the list of those whose help I treasure I must first mention Katie Clarke whose patience, method and attention to detail have been essential as she proof-read my dreadful one-finger typing.

I would also like to thank Steve Georgiou of AT&T, Judi Harper of Swindon College, Ryk Heber of Heber Training Services and Jon Parsons of Brann Direct Marketing for their help and encouragement as they cast a professional eye over the manuscript and for their observations which I have tried to incorporate.

Lastly I would like to express my appreciation and thanks to Michael Armstrong for supporting me when the book was hardly a gleam in anyone's eye, for his restraining some of my wilder flights of fancy and for the time he has taken to write the foreword and to make valuable suggestions for inclusion in the book.

David Turner
Tetbury, Gloucestershire
Autumn 1992

Foreword

Over the last decade there have been five major developments in personnel and training management: the arrival of human resource management (HRM), the competency movement, the emphasis on performance, the importance attached to process as distinct from systems and procedures and, finally, the overriding significance of organizational culture.

HRM is an attitude of mind rather than a set of techniques. Its message is that employees should be treated as assets to be developed rather than controlled. It is essentially a management-driven activity, allocating to line managers the responsibility for achieving continuous improvement in the performance of their staff.

The competency movement has been criticized by people like Professor John Burgoyne because of the dubious underlying assumption that the concept of total competence can be broken down into lists of managerial competencies that purport to be relatively universal and easily measurable. But the concept of competence, which can be defined as the willingness and ability to perform a task or the behaviourial dimensions that affect job performance, is a useful one. It stresses that, when developing the ability of managers to perform their work, we are not just concerned with their knowledge and skills but also with their behaviour – how they get things done and make things happen.

The emphasis on performance in terms not just of output and results but also of total quality has led to the introduction of performance management systems, the essence of which is their developmental nature – the creation of a situation in which there is continuous dialogue between managers and their staff about the behaviour required of both parties in order to improve performance. The performance movement has also led to the introduction of many ill-conceived and badly managed performance-related pay schemes which have failed to motivate. Increasing the level of motivation and commitment is more a matter of managers working effectively with their staff than the use of a mechanical pay-for-performance system.

Next, there is the importance attached to process, which can be defined as the way things are done in an organization – how people behave and interact and how systems and procedures are operated. What matters is not the elegance of the system or procedure but the manner in which management puts it to use.

Process is the 'way things are done around here' aspect of culture. But that is how culture manifests itself. What is more important is to understand the norms and values which underpin the culture and which have to be understood if behaviour is to be changed in any way. These five developments are each concerned with different aspects of behaviour and raise the important question of how behaviour is modified in order to improve performance and overall effectiveness.

Fundamentally, of course, people's behaviour at work is shaped by their experience of working for managers, with colleagues and within the culture of the organization. Some people can learn effectively in this way, most need some help so that they can understand how to make better use of their knowledge and skills. Again, a good manager within the context of a good performance management system, can provide the guidance and coaching required. But this demands considerable skill which has to be learned.

HRM, competence development, performance improvement and process and culture management all require inter-personal skills and these can be enhanced in training programmes – formal courses, workshops or small 'improvement groups' operating within departments. The trainer – who could be a line manager with the right sort of skills – is essentially a facilitator. He or she helps people to understand more about how they behave at work and how they can modify that behaviour to good purpose.

It is in this area of continuous development that role playing exercises can play an important part. They give those involved the opportunity to practise their skills in an unthreatening atmosphere in which they are given every opportunity to learn for themselves.

As someone who has been involved in management training for many years and has introduced role plays on numerous occasions I welcome David Turner's book, which gives clear guidance on how to get the best out of role playing and a wide range of exercises that can be used as written, or modified to suit the circumstances of the organization.

Michael Armstrong
Independent Consultant

Role play summaries

NEGOTIATION

1: The building site

Approx time required: Up to 3 hours
Numbers involved: 5 plus observers
Skills practised: General negotiation skills, defining strategies and identifying the other side's interests, gaining agreement to mutually advantageous solutions, the resolution of conflict and negotiating as the representative of a group.

This role play, which is set outside most people's working experience, is written around a situation in which residents of a road close to a large development have plenty to complain about. The company whose development it is has acquired rapid, and maybe dubious, planning permission and is desperate to finish the work quickly. Safety, noise, dirt and behaviour are all issues. The Residents' Committee is negotiating for the residents. This should allow plenty of scope for emotions to surface and lessons in controlling them to be brought out. The need to concentrate on facts to produce constructive results can be demonstrated and there are opportunities for creative solutions to be worked out.

2: The youth club

Approx time required: Up to 2 hours
Numbers involved: 3 plus observers
Skills practised: General negotiation skills, defining strategies,

creating and gaining agreement to mutually advantageous solutions, identifying the interests of others, dealing with conflict and
emotion.

This role play, in a youth club setting, concentrates on the youth
club leader, who is keen to retain the reputation of the club, and
irate neighbours who want some reparation for damage caused by
vandals who may or may not have been club members. Creative
solutions are called for and the ongoing relationship with the
neighbours is important for the club leader.

3: The packaging purchase

Approx time required: Up to $1\frac{1}{2}$ hours
Numbers involved: 2 plus observers
Skills practised: General negotiation skills, identifying one's own
and the other side's interests, recognition of the importance of other
issues as well as price, constructing and achieving agreement to
mutually advantageous solutions.

A role play to practise bargaining over price, service and conditions
of sale. The buyer is from a giftware manufacturer keen to arrange
supplies of a packaging item for the coming year. Quality and service
are important and the supplier has always been reliable. The
supplier's rep must try and negotiate a price increase higher than
inflation – or is there another solution?

4: Renting factory space

Approx time required: Up to $1\frac{1}{4}$ hours
Numbers involved: 2 plus observers
Skills practised: General negotiation skills, defining strategies,
identifying others' interests, obtaining mutually advantageous
agreements, recognition of the importance of factors other than
price.

This role play covers a simple rental agreement for factory space
and is designed to provide the opportunity for some creative
bargaining. The owner's agent wishes to impose restrictions on the
use of the space and to get a good rent, the tenant is stretched
financially and wants a good price.

5: Sharing equipment

Approx time required: Up to 1¼ hours
Numbers involved: 2 plus observers
Skills practised: General negotiation skills, defining strategies, identifying others' interests, obtaining mutually advantageous agreements.

A small business builds and sells kit cars for others under contract. Testing and tuning equipment would be very useful but very expensive. The dealer in second-hand cars next door has a small workshop and might be prepared to share costs. The negotiation is to decide the details of a possible deal.

6: Maintenance or production?

Approx time required: Up to 1½ hours
Numbers involved: 2 plus observers
Skills practised: General negotiation skills, identifying common interests and aims, generating mutually acceptable solutions.

Two managers must come to an agreement over the redecoration of a working site. The programme, which may disrupt operations or cost too much, must be a compromise between cost and operational efficiency.

7: Neighbourly exchange

Approx time required: Up to 1 hour
Numbers involved: 2 plus observers
Skills practised: General negotiation skills, identifying common interests, constructing creative and mutually agreeable solutions.

Two neighbours each have something to offer the other if they can only discover how to go about it. Can they agree on the best method of exchange to mutual advantage?

8: The gravel pits

Approx time required: Up to 2½ hours
Numbers involved: 4 plus observers
Skills practised: General negotiation skills, identifying common and

conflicting interests, constructing creative and mutually advantageous solutions.

The owners of some derelict land wish to sell it to realize its value. The local authority, a small leisure company and conservationists are all interested in the land for different purposes. There needs to be a general agreement on the way forward. Negotiations can be carried out in different groups or at a single conference or both. A whole range of different solutions are possible.

APPRAISAL

9: The faltering section

Approx time required: Up to 2 hours
Numbers involved: 2 plus observers
Skills practised: General appraisal interviewing skills, exploring attitudes and perceptions, handling criticism and emotion, gaining acceptance of the need for change, making and agreeing firm plans for action.

George Williams has been recruited to run a new section which is not performing as well as was expected. His trade skills are good, although some changes in his practices may be necessary, but his attitudes to his staff and the example he sets require attention.

10: The zealous employee

Approx time required: Up to 1½ hours
Numbers involved: 2 plus observers
Skills practised: General appraisal interviewing skills, probing underlying causes of behaviour, sensitivity to others' feelings, setting standards and agreeing firm action plans.

Mary Holden is an older keyboard operator with a problem of relating to younger members of staff and to her new young supervisor. She is a good worker who is disruptive and who may be having problems with the new systems.

11: The employee near retirement

Approx time required: Up to 1¼ hours
Numbers involved: 2 plus observers
Skills practised: General appraisal interviewing skills, the remotivation of an employee near to retirement, exploring attitudes and perceptions and agreeing firm action plans.

Harold Brown is 58 and has achieved a comfortable position in life. He is content to coast for the next few years until retirement. The team cannot afford a passenger and the appraising manager needs to remotivate him to take a full and active part in the team's activities.

12: Competence without confidence

Approx time required: Up to 1½ hours
Numbers involved: 2 plus observers
Skills practised: General appraisal interviewing skills, the use of self appraisal, exploring attitudes and perceptions, agreeing plans for future conduct.

Chris has recently been promoted to run the giftware section in this retail operation. So far there has been evidence of good performance but there is a lack of confidence and an unwillingness to contribute ideas.

13: The uncommitted warehouseman

Approx time required: Up to 1½ hours
Numbers involved: 2 plus observers
Skills practised: General appraisal interviewing skills, the use of self appraisal, setting standards and gaining agreement to them. The identification of appropriate means to motivate low performing individuals.

A feckless, uncommitted worker with no real awareness of what is required of him, John's appraisal should provide a good chance to spell out the error of his ways and set standards. Finding a 'hook' to motivate him to perform better may prove difficult.

14: The brilliant technician

Approx time required: Up to 1½ hours
Numbers involved: 2 plus observers
Skills practised: General appraisal interview skills, self appraisal, identifying underlying causes of behaviour, setting goals and agreeing future actions.

Technically brilliant, Michelle is a real asset to the company. However her interpersonal skills are woefully inadequate and she is a disruptive element in the team.

15: The friendly service engineer

Approx time required: Up to 1½ hours
Numbers involved: 2 plus observers
Skills practised: General appraisal interview skills, self appraisal and gaining recognition of the need to change, setting standards and gaining agreement and plans to meet them.

As a service engineer, Steve is only adequate. He is scruffy, disorganized and not too worried about the quality of work that he does. Since the engineer works alone, how can the appraising manager motivate him to change?

16: Hoping for promotion

Approx time required: Up to 1½ hours
Numbers involved: 2 plus observers
Skills practised: General appraisal interview skills, self appraisal to gain acceptance of personal limitations, the identification of means of motivating particular individuals.

Pat is a very capable but difficult sales office manager, who has reached the limit as far as promotion is concerned. Pat is still ambitious and the appraising manager needs to find some way of maintaining the good performance without advancement.

17: The frustrated high flyer

Approx time required: Up to 1½ hours
Numbers involved: 2 plus observers

Skills practised: General appraisal interview skills, generation of creative plans to motivate and retain the individual, probing underlying behaviour and agreeing future plans.

This employee is excellent, a very high performer. He is able, conscientious and with lots of potential. He is looking for a challenging role at a time of personal uncertainty but the organization has no suitable slot for him at the moment.

DISCIPLINE

18: The bad timekeeper

Approx time required: Up to 1½ hours
Numbers involved: 3 or 4 plus observers
Skills practised: General discipline interviewing skills, the careful establishment of the facts and agreeing the standards required for the future.

This role play concerns a manager wishing to discipline an employee for bad timekeeping. The setting can be almost any you choose except situations where staff are required to use a time clock or work shifts. The scenario could be rewritten and adjusted to take account of 'clocking in'. The employee in question has a series of domestic problems, about which he/she is unwilling to speak, which make it very difficult to be on time every day. There is plenty of scope for the procedures used in your organization to be applied to this situation.

19: Gross misconduct?

Approx time required: Up to 1½ hours
Numbers involved: 4 plus observers
Skills practised: General disciplinary interviewing skills, establishing facts, judgement and listening to all sides of the case.

This role play concerns an employee accused of theft having apparently been caught red-handed. He is not popular with his foreman, who is accusing him, and he is a recent arrival. The manager is faced with evidence and denials. The sequence of events is not in dispute. He is forced into considering whether the employee's intention was to steal or not. Should this case lead to dismissal?

20: The bad back

Approx time required: Up to 1½ hours
Numbers involved: 2 plus observers
Skills practised: General interviewing skills, identifying the facts, separating sickness from absence, defining clear standards for future behaviour and ensuring the consequences of non-compliance are understood.

In this role play the managing director must address the unfortunate situation in which a long-serving and valued employee has had to take considerable time off through a back injury. This has been going on for some time and is no longer acceptable. The team is constantly one short or the company has had to pay temps as well as statutory and company sick pay.

21: The poor performer

Approx time required: Up to 1 hour
Numbers involved: 2 plus observers
Skills practised: General interviewing skills, setting standards for future behaviour, establishing the facts, ensuring the consequences of non-compliance are understood.

This role play concerns a situation in which an employee has failed consistently to perform to an adequate standard. Despite several attempts by the supervisor and the manager to coach and encourage, results have not improved. A formal disciplinary hearing is called for.

22: The second offence

Approx time required: Up to 1½ hours
Numbers involved: 4 plus observers
Skills practised: General interviewing skills, establishing the facts, ensuring understanding of previous disciplinary action, defining standards for the future and ensuring that the consequences of a failure to meet them are understood.

This case concerns a written warning that has been issued to an employee and now he has done the same thing again. Do you issue a final warning or are there extenuating circumstances? The original warning letter forms part of the brief.

23: The Christmas lunch

Approx time required: Up to 1½ hours
Numbers involved: 4 plus observers
Skills practised: General interviewing skills, judgement, establishing facts, even handed dealings with employee and supervisor.

The annual Christmas lunch at this factory is the occasion for an employee to fall out with his supervisor and swing a punch at him. Who was to blame, and where did the drink come from? Should the manager deal with the supervisor as well?

24: Accident-prone or careless?

Approx time required: Up to 1¼ hours
Numbers involved: 2 or 4 plus observers
Skills practised: General interviewing skills, establishing the facts, gaining acceptance of the need to improve, defining standards for the future.

A fork-lift truck driver has a history of small accidents. One more accident, involving an injury, prompts the manager to speak to the driver with the intention of improving his driving.

25: Failure to meet targets

Approx time required: Up to 1½ hours
Numbers involved: 2 plus observers
Skills practised: General interviewing skills, establishing the facts, gaining acceptance of the need to improve, defining standards and spelling out the next steps if no improvement is noted.

A salesman targeted with a perfectly achievable level of sales has consistently failed to reach the sales required. Several attempts to coach and assist have failed to produce results. A formal warning that he needs to reach the targets seems to be the only option left to his sales manager. And anyway, why are his results so poor?

GRIEVANCE

26: The missed promotion

Approx time required: Up to 1¼ hours
Numbers involved: 2 plus observers
Skills practised: General interviewing skills, gaining acceptance for decisions, exploring attitudes and perceptions, dealing with emotion and finding creative solutions to resolve grievances.

This scenario concerns a manager who was temporarily promoted to the position of workshop manager and anticipated that it would become a permanent situation. When this did not occur he feels aggrieved and takes the complaint to his boss.

27: The loss of overtime

Approx time required: Up to 1 hour
Numbers involved: 2 plus observers
Skills practised: General interviewing skills, exploration of attitudes and perceptions, dealing with emotion and gaining acceptance of unpopular decisions.

An employee with a medical condition that might be exacerbated by the work is refused a share of the overtime that is available.

28: Poor working conditions

Approx time required: Up to 1½ hours
Numbers involved: 3 plus observers
Skills practised: General interviewing skills, exploration of attitudes and perceptions, establishing trust, gaining acceptance and cooperation.

The local union official becomes involved when a whole factory is disrupted by building work that goes wrong. Working conditions deteriorate and the management appear to have done little to keep staff informed or working happily despite the obvious difficulties.

29: The change of offices

Approx time required: Up to 1¼ hours
Numbers involved: 2 plus observers

Skills practised: General interviewing skills, assessing the real causes, dealing with emotion and resentment, establishing trust and giving reassurance.

A manager, returning from a slightly prolonged holiday, finds that his office has been moved to a mean little room, his secretary is now to be shared with the person who has his old office and he didn't even know that there was to be a new appointment made.

30: Persecution?

Approx time required: Up to 2 hours
Numbers involved: 3 plus observers
Skills practised: General interviewing skills, dealing with emotion and resentment, gaining acceptance for decisions taken.

A young employee feels that he has been consistently unfairly treated by his supervisor. The supervisor believes the employee to be a time waster and that he fails to pull his weight.

31: Paying for qualifications

Approx time required: Up to 1 hour
Numbers involved: 2 plus observers
Skills practised: General interviewing skills, selling benefits and advantages to overcome objections, searching for individual motivational needs and devising ways of meeting them.

A committed member of staff is trapped by an inflexible salary and grading system. Another staff member, better qualified but less good at the job, is on a higher grade.

MANAGING PEOPLE AT WORK

32: The under-achiever

Approx time required: Up to 1½ hours
Numbers involved: 2 plus observers
Skills practised: General interviewing skills, gaining agreement and commitment to change, dealing with emotion and resentment of criticism, agreeing plans and targets for improvement.

A young employee, well qualified, is consistently failing to produce the required standard of work. The problem would appear to be a lack of application and an unwillingness to give work a high enough priority in life.

33: Breaking the bad news

Approx time required: Up to 1¼ hours
Numbers involved: 2 plus observers
Skills practised: General interviewing skills, dealing with emotion and resentment, finding ways of continuing to motivate staff, practising sensitive approaches to difficult situations.

A very ambitious production manager was widely tipped to be the next production director when the present one retires. The new appointment has been made but not yet announced and the manager has to be told that he has not got the job.

34: Delegating a project

Approx time required: Up to 1½ hours
Numbers involved: 2 plus observers
Skills practised: General interviewing skills, approaching and 'selling' a delegation, gaining agreement and commitment, agreeing plans and time scales for the transfer period.

A bright young trainee who is doing very well with her accountancy exams is becoming bored with the routine duties she has to perform. The boss decides to give her a project that will stretch her and give her something she can submit towards her qualification.

35: Selling ideas to the boss

Approx time required: Up to 1¼ hours
Numbers involved: 2 plus observers
Skills practised: General interviewing skills, choosing an approach appropriate to the person addressed, selling benefits and bargaining, influencing skills.

A manager with a plan for investment to improve the working environment, and thus productivity and staff motivation, must convince her boss of the need and value of it.

36: **Persuading the doubter**

Approx time required: Up to 1½ hours
Numbers involved: 2 plus observers
Skills practised: General interviewing skills, tailoring the approach to the individual, clarification and understanding of objections, selling benefits and approaches to the management of change.

A manager has grave doubts about the wisdom of a proposed course of action to establish a consultative committee with the workforce. The manager who proposed it has to sell the idea. In short, the conflict of views is centred over the relationship of staff and management and over the management of change.

37: **Mistakes have been made**

Approx time required: Up to 1 hour
Numbers involved: 2 plus observers
Skills practised: General interviewing skills, avoiding offensive/defensive behaviour, resolving differences constructively, agreeing ways for future cooperation.

Two managers meet to discuss a failure in the area of control of one of them. There is a need to retain working relationships, improve for the future and avoid recriminations.

38: **Mid-career crisis**

Approx time required: Up to 1 hour
Numbers involved: 2 plus observers
Skills practised: General interviewing skills, crystallizing thoughts and ideas, encouraging self appraisal and reflection, the avoidance of promises that cannot be kept.

A manager is unsure of where his career is going. He seeks advice from his boss about the prospects and possibilities within the current organization.

39: **The thorn in the flesh**

Approx time required: Up to 1 hour
Numbers involved: 2 plus observers

Skills practised: General interviewing skills, encouraging self appraisal and reflection, gaining acceptance of a need for change and making plans for it.

A manager, who is competent in many ways, lacks confidence in his own ability to act but repeatedly criticizes the actions of others. He has all the answers but seems unable to apply them practically. Unwilling to compromise, he seems to upset people every time he tries to do anything.

40: The resented promotion

Approx time required: Up to 1 hour
Numbers involved: 2 plus observers
Skills practised: General interviewing skills, dealing with emotion and conflict, encouraging reflection and self analysis, assertiveness and controlling conversations.

A newly promoted supervisor decides he must address the problem of the resentment one of his new team feels towards his promotion.

FIVE-MINUTE ROLE PLAYS

For all the following role plays:

Approx time required: Up to 15 minutes
Numbers involved: 2 plus observers (except number 60 which requires 3).
Skills practised: General interviewing skills including questioning, listening, assertiveness and controlling conversations. Each role play may also raise other, more specific, issues.

41: The lunchtime celebrations

Misunderstandings abound after the supervisor comes back late from lunch.

42: The early finisher

Why does this man always pack up early? It is beginning to rub off on others.

43: Why can't he work overtime?

This man's skills are critical to the operation working over a Bank Holiday. He has arranged to take his family away for the weekend, having worked too many weekends already.

44: Thwarted ambitions

This is a case of someone who felt that they had been promised promotion – and then didn't get it.

45: The late report

The report is not ready when promised. No real excuse is offered and there was no warning that it would be late.

46: The temporary transfer

Help is urgently required in the neighbouring section. The only person available to help is very busy and does not want to move.

47: The scruffy salesman

A successful salesman is careless of his dress and comments have been made by clients. He also had a row with a customer the other day. The company's reputation and image are suffering.

48: Old hand – new manager

The new young manager on his third day in office has arranged to meet one of the managers reporting to him. This manager, an older man with long service, resents a younger man and is determined to keep him out of his patch.

49: The committee member

The chairman of a local voluntary organization's committee has a committee member who attends very irregularly and when consulted will always argue against any change. This member is a real obstacle to progress.

50: Can he take a holiday?

A last-minute panic puts an executive's paid-up holiday in jeopardy.

51: Praise and develop

A young manager has just completed a project with an excellent outcome. His manager wishes to praise him and discuss future development.

52: The transfer

An employee, who is a key member of the section and ready for promotion, applies for a transfer and promotion in a neighbouring department. Can the manager persuade the employee to stay?

53: The wandering maintenance man

The manager of a small satellite site relies on a maintenance service provided by the maintenance team at the main site. The one man allocated never seems to be there. The site manager approaches the maintenance manager to try to assert more control.

54: Allocating an unpopular job

A supervisor has to tell a member of his staff that they have to help set up a trade show stand, a job that no one wants.

55: Personal hygiene

One employee is upsetting the others with a personal hygiene problem. The supervisor needs to do something about it.

56: The coffee circle

The managers of a small organization and their secretaries have taken to having coffee and a chat at the start of their day. The administration staff in the office alongside find it distracting and upsetting.

57: The affair at work

Two members of staff are having an affair. The husband of one of them begins to suspect and appears at the manager's home, at the weekend, to try to discover the truth.

58: Conflicting interests

A workshop manager needs some equipment for maintenance before a statutory inspection and the operations manager has failed to arrange for it to be free. A conflict of interests and a systems failure are apparent.

59: Seeking opinion

A manager wants to promote an employee and seeks the opinion of the candidate's current supervisor – who dislikes this individual.

60: Customer complaint

A young assistant deals badly with an old and valued customer who has come in to complain. Voices are raised and the manager intervenes.

PART 1

USING ROLE PLAYS

Chapter 1:

An introduction to role playing

This book is designed to be a sourcebook of role play scenarios for busy trainers. The situations and scenarios included describe aspects of communication and face-to-face communication in particular. It is in this area of inter-personal communication skills that role playing can be amazingly successful in changing both behaviour and attitudes.

WHO IS IT FOR?

The book is written with a wide range of potential users in mind. Those who may find material of interest and use include trainers who are involved in:

- management skills;
- supervisory skills;
- inter-personal skills in a work context;
- management and staff development;
- business training in colleges and business schools.

It is intended as a resource offering relevant situations and scenarios to use to explore the effectiveness of different types of behaviour by people at work, particularly by those who manage others.

HOW TO USE THIS BOOK

Part 1, the first 3 chapters, is intended as a reminder of the principal characteristics of role playing, its use and the skills involved for trainers and trainees alike. It contains a certain amount of practical guidance for those unfamiliar with the necessary techniques. Read, browse or select particular topics at will. This part also includes some copiable notes and checklists for trainers and players for use with any or all the role play scenarios.

Chapter 3 contains some thoughts about how trainers might extend the use of role plays and use them in more unusual ways. It deals with the techniques involved in writing their own situations; here trainers should find some tips on producing effective role plays for themselves.

The chapters in Part 2 contain groups of scenarios focusing on particular skill areas that are suitably addressed by the medium of role plays. The role plays are set in a variety of environments and the skill areas covered are:

* negotiation;
* appraisal;
* discipline;
* grievance;
* managing people at work.

The role plays in chapters 4 to 8 are longer ones requiring between 1 and 3 hours to play out. There are some 40 scenarios in total of this type in the book which are intended for use as major items in training events. With every role play there are some basic notes for the trainer and specific briefing notes for each participant, which are intended to be photo-copied. Each role player should receive only their own brief and any other general papers: they should not be told what is in other briefs. The trainer's notes give an indication of the numbers of participants involved, the time required and the equipment needed. They also describe the range of learning points that should emerge, and skills practised, and some suggestions for questions that could be answered in the review phase.

Chapter 9 is different, in that it has a range of very simple pen pictures of familiar situations which can be played out very quickly and reviewed like their longer and more complex cousins in the other chapters. These are intended for inclusion in training events, for small subsidiary groups to play out among themselves, or for use on the spur of the moment, if a situation arises in which the trainer would like to see some activity tried out. They can also be used very effectively to familiarize people with role playing and to remove anxieties that they may have about it.

WHAT IS A ROLE PLAY?

A role play, used for training purposes, is a simulation in which trainees are required to act out the role of an individual in a situation or in circumstances that are relevant to the trainee. The scenario can be an imaginary one or a real situation that the trainee is shortly to face.

In practice, most role plays take the form of a one-act, unscripted playlet involving 2 or more participants taking the parts of different people.

THE PURPOSE OF ROLE PLAY

Role playing is a valuable technique for the trainer. It can provide participation, involvement and the opportunity for action learning. Participants act out (or practise) real life situations (or situations that could occur in real life) in a protected environment. Their behaviour, speech and feelings during the playlet form the basis for self appraisal and feedback from others who have been observing; from this they will learn which behaviour, words and approaches are effective. Mistakes can be made and learned from in a risk-free way.

Role playing during training permits participants to receive objective feedback about their performance from their peers and from the trainer. They can learn what others see and hear and feel. Trainees can discover the impact their attitudes and behaviour have in terms of how effective they are perceived to be by others. This opportunity to receive feedback rarely, if ever, occurs in normal circumstances back at work.

Role playing can provide a mirror for participants to see themselves as others see them. This encourages insight into their own behaviour and sensitivity to others' opinions, attitudes and needs. The benefits of a change in behaviour or attitude can readily be demonstrated and thus any desired change is encouraged.

WHEN TO USE A ROLE PLAY

Since role plays are most effective as vehicles in which to practise or learn face-to-face communication skills they are most suitable for use where participants can practise ways to deal with individuals and their problems. For the trainer, role plays provide a good way to involve trainees actively and intensively in a training session, helping them to learn in a more active and participative way.

Occasions for using a role play:

- Where the need is to practise effective communication and inter-personal skills. Examples of these situations are negotiation, performance appraisal and disciplinary interviews.
- As an opportunity for the trainer to involve trainees intensively in the learning process.
- As an opportunity to practise approaches to forthcoming real life situations.
- As an opportunity to replay a situation that was not successfully handled in the past in order to extract lessons for the future.
- Where a change of attitude is desirable. Trainees can come to appreciate the viewpoint of another person or group if they are asked to take part in a role play in the role of that person or as a member of that group.

LEARNING FROM ROLE PLAY

Regardless of the precise situation, there are many common lessons to be learnt. These are in the area of effective face-to-face communication. The manager's ability to coach, influence, persuade, advise or fully understand is crucial to the successful conduct of the interview or conversation whether the subject at issue is negotiation or handling grievances. Similarly, the value of effective questioning and listening is fundamental to all management and workplace communication, as is an awareness and recognition of body language. All these aspects of face-to-face communication skills can be easily addressed by role playing. The ability to control conversations, handle conflict, reach agreement or gain commitment can also be improved through role playing. In addition, changes in attitude and perception are often the result of playing the role of someone else.

More specific points that may emerge from the individual role plays in this book are described in the introduction with each scenario.

POTENTIAL DRAWBACKS

The principal drawback of role playing is that it is open to criticism for lack of realism. It is unlikely that a role play will accurately depict all the complexities that arise at work. Inevitably, therefore, it can be criticized for being simplistic and thus lose credibility.

In its defence, any technique that can give trainees the confidence to try new approaches (that have been endorsed by their peers and the trainer as being likely to be effective) must be worth using. Certainly, no role play can foresee all eventualities in a situation but many of the concerns and problems can be anticipated and effective behaviours to deal with them devised.

A further concern about role playing is that many people are unwilling to put themselves at the risk of appearing foolish or of making mistakes in public. People often feel threatened by video cameras or the knowledge that their behaviour is under close scrutiny by their peers. These fears can be removed only if all are involved and if everyone has the opportunity to contribute to the feedback on everyone else. An atmosphere of mutual support can be generated very quickly by the trainer who is aware of this problem. The fear of the camera can be reduced by a practice run in which all the shyness can be overcome.

The effectiveness of role playing as a training tool is dependent on the quality of the feedback. Feedback must be constructive or it is counter-productive, saps confidence and erects barriers to learning. Positive and well-handled feedback can reinforce effective behaviour, instil confidence and highlight specific areas for improvement in a way that is not critical and is readily acceptable.

Chapter 2:

Making role plays work

CHOOSING A SCENARIO

The choice of scenario by the trainer should be governed by the need for the role play to contribute to the overall training objectives. Thereafter, the choice is affected by only 3 factors. These are:

- Credibility – the degree to which the situation described is familiar to or recognizable by the intended participants.
- Relevance – the scenario must permit the trainer to extract the learning point(s) required from the situation to be played.
- Level of complexity – this must reflect the experience, education and understanding of the intended participants.

To select a role play from this book it is suggested that the trainer should:

- Decide whether a role play is appropriate and what using it is intended to achieve.
- Choose the subject area. The role plays are grouped into chapters by subject area for ease of access, eg Appraisal, Discipline.
- Consider the particular learning points that need to be emphas-

ized. Each chapter and each role play has some notes about the principal lessons that the scenario is designed to bring out.

- Decide how much time is available. Each role play has an estimate of the time it should take to run.
- Consider numbers. The numbers of participants and the facilities required are described at the front of each scenario.
- Consider the experience and background of the participants and choose a scenario with which they can identify; each role play is described in outline at the front of the book to provide a flavour of its content and assist the choice.

THE WAY TO PLAY

Choosing participants

When first introducing role play to a training event there is bound to be a degree of uncertainty and apprehension among the trainees unless they have previously been involved in role playing. For this reason it is often advisable to choose the most outgoing or confident of the trainees to have the first attempt (or, of course, someone who has done it before). It is sometimes a good idea to try and match people with the role play characters but in many cases playing a character very different from oneself can become a real opportunity to explore others' attitudes and feelings. It is often not necessary, for instance, to find a woman to play a female part, or an older person to play someone nearing retirement. However, to increase participants' comfort on their first go it may be advisable to choose roles that are not too distant from their own.

It is sometimes a valuable technique to use role reversal. For example, the manager about to conduct appraisal interviews can usefully become the appraisee for a short spell and experience the feelings of someone in that position.

Do not be put off by the male or female names in the scenarios. In almost every case the characters could be either male or female and you can readily change the names if they are seen as a barrier.

Making the environment 'safe'

Any role play will induce anxiety, particularly for those who are unfamiliar with the process. To reduce the anxiety levels, there are several things that trainers can do:

- Make sure that everyone is absolutely clear about the aims of the session, what is expected and how the feedback will be conducted. Some notes for role players are on page 48 (Handout 4).
- It must always be emphasized that the role play is an opportunity to learn. It is in no way intended to open anyone to ridicule or humiliation but rather to provide an opportunity from which to learn. There is no competition and no comparisons should be made.
- Everyone in the group must be made aware that they too will be participating. Try and create a cooperative, supportive atmosphere.
- Give instruction on the correct way to give feedback and ensure that all are aware that only constructive criticism is welcome. See notes and drills for giving feedback on pages 45 and 46 (Handouts 1 & 2).
- Give assurances that no reports about the participants' performance will be made and that all video tapes will be wiped clear at the end of the session.
- Select role plays that are readily recognizable as relevant to the participants and start with simple cases that will produce successful outcomes. (Chapter 9 provides a range of simple scenarios which can be used as confidence builders.)
- Participants will feel more comfortable once they have had a chance to get to know the other course members, so run role plays later rather than sooner in the programme.
- Allow the playing individuals to have a supporter or team with whom they confer before the role play and who are able to prompt if the player is going off course or is drying up.
- Reduce the exposure felt by the participants and allow the play to take place in groups of 3: ie, 2 players and an observer. The obvious disadvantage is the difficulty the trainer will have in keeping up with what is happening in several groups at once. (The scenarios in Chapter 9 are very suitable for work with small groups.)

Use of observers

While running role plays there will normally be a number of people who are not directly involved in the action. To involve them more and to enable them, as well as the players, to learn from the role play they can be nominated as observers or supporters (as above). The role of the observer is to:

- Watch the action and to gauge the effectiveness of the participants' behaviour, in order to be able to feed back what was observed. Some conclusions about the effectiveness of what was observed should form part of the review session.
- Remain uninvolved in order to see things that the players do not.
- Raise the learning points for the participants and the rest of the group. A structured observation sheet is a good method of ensuring that the observer is looking for the relevant things. An example of an observation sheet is given on page 47 (Handout 3).

It is possible to ask one observer to watch the non-verbal communication while another is observing the questioning technique. Observers should be made aware of the importance of their role in the learning process for the participants and of the opportunity they themselves have to learn from their close involvement.

The role of observer will take less time to prepare than the one of a participant in a role play. To involve everyone, in a training session in which there are to be several role plays, it may be possible for trainers to brief players for the next role play while the first participants are preparing their roles. This will help to reduce the overall time required by concurrent activity.

REVIEW AND FEEDBACK

On completion of the role play it is essential that players are able to reflect upon what has happened and receive feedback from others. Feedback should be immediate, constructive, very specific and should link behaviour to effectiveness.

The object of feedback is to bring about the awareness of a need for change and to indicate the direction in which the change may most effectively be made. To be effective feedback should:

- Be readily acceptable.
- Be specific – generalizations are useless. It should identify specific detail and the effect it caused, ie it should link behaviour to performance.
- Avoid judgements and speculation. It should stick to observable facts and their effect.
- Be balanced – it is as important to be aware of what worked well as it is to become aware of what worked less well.
- Suggest alternative courses of action for consideration. Beware 'should do' and use 'could do'.

If it is effective, feedback will ensure that the recipient:

- can understand it;
- can agree with it;
- will be ready to modify their behaviour;
- will know how to go about changing it.

Some notes on a format for giving feedback and on a review procedure are given later in this chapter. See pages 45 and 46 (Handouts 1 & 2).

Use of video recording and playback equipment

The recording of role plays using video equipment can be very valuable. There is an immediate record to refer to and from which to draw 'action replays' during the review. The players themselves have the chance to observe their behaviour in action and draw conclusions in the same way as the observers. The video recording overcomes the problem of differences of recall; it records what actually happened. It also records very clearly all the important and revealing non-verbal behaviour – the body language.

It is usually best to take the self appraisal part of the review and one or two major observations from the rest of the group before playing back the video. This will focus attention on the areas of most concern. The trainer should be prepared to stop, rewind and replay particular sequences of importance or to fast forward over digressions and irrelevancies. The replay of the whole of a long role play can be very time consuming. It should be possible to note events of significance as they occur by elapsed time, or by the counter on the recorder, so that the trainer can be selective in what is played back. This helps to reinforce the feedback already given. As a general rule, however, it is advisable to allow the players to watch and comment upon as much of the play as possible.

For the purpose of recording, a camera on a tripod manipulated as necessary by the trainer or a member of the group is better than having a hand-held camera: it causes less distraction.

Video recording does have the drawback of tending to make people camera shy and selfconscious. It can also be 'painful' to see and hear oneself recorded for the first time – dearly held self perceptions are sometimes challenged. Trainers can help by using their own first experiences as an example and, by introducing the use of the camera in unchallenging circumstances (for example a group discussion or a group exercise), accustom the group to its presence. People become used to the presence of the camera very quickly.

STANDARD HANDOUT 1
A format for giving feedback

1. A general impression of the overall performance. Was it successful?

2. What went well?
   Give evidence of the major items. For impact restrict the number of points to two or three.

3. What did not go so well?
   Give evidence of the major items. Again, for impact stick to the most important points.

4. Try to get participants to suggest (or failing that, you suggest) possible alternative ways of approaching the problem that may be more effective.

5. Summarize and check understanding.

STANDARD HANDOUT 2
A drill for feedback/review sessions

1. Participants give their views on how it went. Did they achieve what they wanted to? Did they feel it was successful? What were their feelings at different points?

Self appraisal in this way often brings out points that have not gone well without a third party (observer or trainer) having to be critical. People are often harder on their own performance than is necessary: if this happens the feedback from the rest of the group immediately starts on a positive note – 'it really wasn't as bad as you think because …' Most important, self appraisal is the best opportunity for the recognition of a need to change. The points raised should be discussed.

2. Take specific comments from the observers and then from other group members. The trainer controls this feedback, getting everyone as far as possible to have a say and limiting each contribution to a small number of points.

The process of observing and feeding back to the players by the observer(s) helps both groups to learn.

3. Participants should be encouraged to listen to all the feedback before being asked to comment on it.

4. Trainers should first bring out any major points that have been missed, then they should summarize the whole. They should:

   - Concentrate on the learning points they wish to bring out.
   - Try to get away from what happened to explore the effect of particular events and behaviours.
   - Congratulate and thank the participants for their efforts.

STANDARD HANDOUT 3
Role play observation sheet

Note both positive and negative observations below.

Points to consider	Examples and their effect

Opening
    Putting at ease.
    Venue, seating, formality.
    Clarity; was the purpose explained?	

Middle
    Sensitivity, use of questions, listening.
    Control of pace.
    Structure and direction.
    Body language; approach and style.
    Rapport and agreement.
    Who is doing all the talking?	

Ending
    Outcome, feelings at the end, acceptance or agreement.
    Summary.
Overall effectiveness
    Was the aim achieved?	

STANDARD HANDOUT 4
Notes for role players

As you are about to take part in a role play, there are a few guidelines that it would be useful to note. These should help you to learn as much as possible from this session.

1. You are not being asked to be an actor or to entertain. The purpose of the role play is to provide a situation in which you can practise certain skills. When you read the brief, try to imagine yourself in the situation described and behave in a way you feel to be natural – but be conscious of the fact that your role may require a different approach from that which you might normally use.

2. You (and others) may benefit from the chance to experiment with different approaches and behaviour so try to use the approach you feel to be most appropriate for the circumstances described in your brief.

3. The brief is just the starting point. It simply sets the scene. Try not to keep referring to the brief as this will affect the spontaneity of the meeting. Allow the role to develop as you think it might in real life and change your reactions in line with the behaviour and responses of others involved.

4. If you find that you have too little information to answer questions or to describe what has happened in the situation, do feel free to add your own thoughts and ideas. Try to keep these within the framework of the role you are taking and try to make your improvisations realistic.

Checklist: Conducting a role play

1. Explain the purpose of the session and of the role play in particular. Outline the skills that should be practised.
2. Select and reassure participants and put them at ease with the idea of role playing.
3. Issue role play briefs as appropriate, notes for role players (Handout 4, page 48) if required and allow sufficient time for preparation. This is usually detailed in the notes for each role play.
4. Select observers, brief them on what is required and issue a checksheet (Handout 3, page 47, for an example) as well as copies of the briefs issued to participants.
5. Encourage participants to get into role and improvise within the framework of the brief.
6. Check that everyone understands their role and their part in the exercise. Be prepared to answer questions and give clarification.
7. Start the role play and allow it to continue until a reasonable conclusion is reached, until the players dry up or there appears to be no further progress to be made or learning to be acquired. In the event of a breakdown it may be possible to pause, take stock and then continue.
8. Review the process. Allow players the first say, followed by the observers. The trainer will need to control and direct the discussion to cover the main learning points. The principal points that should emerge from the role play are listed in the notes for each role play. (See Handouts 1 & 2, pages 45 & 46).
9. The trainer should close with a summary of what worked well, what were the principal lessons and the areas for all to concentrate on for the future.

Chapter 3:

Other aspects of role play and writing your own

In Chapters 1 and 2 we examined the processes, techniques, advantages and problems of role playing as a medium for training in one-to-one communication skills at work. In this chapter, we shall look at some of the other opportunities that role plays can offer trainers and at how trainers can write specific scenarios to suit their particular requirements and so enhance the way that trainees respond to role playing.

OTHER USES OF ROLE PLAY

Beyond communication skills training the other opportunities presented by role playing include:

- Presenting information. A prepared playlet or role play can be a very powerful and memorable way of imparting information. For example, the impact of a new set of guidelines can be demonstrated with one of the players asking those questions that the audience are likely to want to ask.
- Changing attitudes. Putting people in unfamiliar roles to act out and experience the feelings of, for instance, a person from a

different racial group, can radically alter their perspective and attitudes.

- Exploring attitudes. It is possible to attract feedback and to assess others' reactions to your attitudes and your approach by playing out a situation. It starts to answer the question 'What if I did . . .?'
- Providing a model of behaviour. A role play can be a demonstration of the behaviour that is required and that can be emulated. Examples might be a sales call, dealing with a customer or even the giving of feedback.
- Rehearsal. Role playing can provide the opportunity to rehearse an approach to a situation that one is about to face, or to practise behaviour before using it 'for real' on the customer, the employee, the patient, etc.
- Enhancing self-awareness and sensitivity. Exposure to feedback and the views and feelings of others can help to modify one's behaviour by providing an insight into its effects on others.

Role playing itself is a variable medium. We have examined in Chapters 1 and 2 the use of structured, prepared role plays of variable length as major elements in a learning programme. In some instances the inclusion in a programme of a prepared role play may be inappropriate, particularly in a more learner-centred workshop or session. In these circumstances it may be more appropriate to use specific concerns or situations from the trainees' own workplace to increase the direct relevance of the practice. This will also avoid possible criticism for using material to which trainees have difficulty in relating or recognizing as relevant.

DIFFERENT WAYS TO PLAY

The forms that role plays can take are many and various; the ingenuity of the trainer is the only limitation. There are, however, several well tried methods. These include:

- informal role playing;
- the demonstration role play;
- small group role play;

- whole group role play;
- role reversal;
- spontaneous role play.

Informal role playing

The opportunity to play out a situation may arise in several different ways. A group member may be laying down the law about how something should be done. The trainer can intervene with, 'That sounds interesting. Shall we try it out? You be the . . ., and you take the part of the . . ., and let's see what happens'. This is a very effective way of proving or disproving chairbound statements or advice. The group member who says, 'If I were the boss I would . . .', can be asked to play it out and actually face the situation at issue. The trainer can opt to play one role if a particular behaviour can best be demonstrated in that way or ask someone else to play the second role. It would also be possible to practise role reversal (see below).

The opportunity could also arise from a group member's own situation, 'I have someone at work who . . .'. They can be asked to elaborate on the situation, which is then discussed at large before it is played out using one or more of the approaches emerging from the discussions.

The trainer, who should be alert for these sorts of signals, can readily introduce a role play to provide added opportunities for learning to take place. Chapter 9 provides some short role plays that might be used in this way. These would impose a little more structure, but will provide a 'menu' of scenarios for the trainer to have available in case of need. The notes for trainers in that chapter give some more hints on this.

The demonstration role play

At its simplest the demonstration role play takes the form of a model for others to emulate. It can provide the 'right answer' to a particular situation and, in later practice using different cases, the participants strive to achieve as good a result as in the demonstration. The weakness of this training method is the obvious one of leaving participants with only one way of behaving and the impression that there is only one right way. It can, however, provide a useful introduction to role playing. Most usefully it can demonstrate, in general terms, the type of behaviour that is required and stimulate discussion about the effectiveness of it.

Small group role play

It is possible to break up a large group into smaller ones and run the same role plays in separate groups simultaneously. This gives a range of advantages:

- A larger number of people are more closely involved at all times. More people are actually playing than observing and so large groups can still become involved in learning by experience.
- Much of the 'threat' of performing before a whole group is removed. This method can be used as a way of starting role playing and making the environment safe.
- A range of different outcomes is possible from the same role play scenario; this will generate discussion about the comparative effectiveness of different approaches in the review by the whole group afterwards.

A group of 3 (a triad) is the most commonly used group size. The members of the triad rotate in turn between observer, player A and player B. There should, on each occasion, be several role plays. Each role play is discussed in the small group and major learning points are brought out to the whole parent group at the end. The trainer will need to move between groups helping, answering questions and picking up some of the principal lessons emerging. The drawbacks are that the trainer will not be able to control all that is going on, there will also be a loss of control of the quality of some of the learning, and the time that different groups take for the exercise will vary. Those that finish first can be asked supplementary questions about their performance.

Whole group role play

This is a very useful technique with maximum involvement. It can be used to debate any issue but is most effective when addressed at some matter internal to the organization that causes concern. It can be used to air differences or to gain consensus. It can take many forms, from a structured debate on a topic about which there is disagreement, to a representative meeting (in which players take the parts of others) to highlight the effects of different behaviours. Decision making, team building and planning strategies for resolving particular problems are examples of areas in which total involvement like this could prove valuable.

The control of such an event can be a daunting prospect for the trainer and should not be attempted by the inexperienced or faint-hearted!

Role reversal

Role reversal is very effective as a technique for improving sensitivity and enhancing self-awareness. For example, a manager required to conduct a disciplinary or appraisal interview is asked to take the place of the employee and go through the process from that angle. The feelings generated are powerful pointers to the identification of both effective and ineffective behaviour. There are many other examples – the doctor plays patient, the salesman plays customer, the probation officer an ex-offender, etc.

Role reversal can be used on its own (to play out a particular situation that has arisen during discussion) or as a way of playing the more structured role plays provided in this book. By occupying the other person's place we become more aware of their needs, attitudes and feelings. It is possible to switch roles during the role play (more than once, if necessary) to prompt some movement if positions become entrenched.

Spontaneous role play

Spontaneous role play is the name given to a technique in which trainees are asked to produce their own situations in which to brief others in the group. These situations are then played out:

- by others in the group;
- by the person whose problem it is, as a rehearsal;
- or as a role reversal.

The learning arises from the discussions and the play (which may be repeated several times to explore different approaches) and in reinforcing earlier lessons.

This technique is a very useful one for starting the process of transferring the learning back to the real world from the classroom. The skills and techniques learned are applied to real problems, in a no-risk situation. The trainees see that the training process can have a very practical application. This method tends to appeal because people are playing either themselves or from their own particular experience.

WRITING YOUR OWN ROLE PLAYS

Naturally, there will be occasions on which you will wish to write your own role plays. This will either be to make the situations more closely relevant to the trainees or because you have been unable to discover any material that would bring out effectively the points you wish to see made.

When considering the subject area, it is best to rely on your own experience and knowledge; this will increase the reality of the situations and enhance their acceptability. You need to consider what lessons you wish to raise and examine your intended scenario with the learning points in mind. You will probably need to produce several scenarios for a given training event and it is worth considering how to vary the complexity of the cases. You can then start with simple situations and move on to the more complex.

With the exception of very simple situations, the characters that you create need a certain amount of flesh. They need to be recognizable and to be put in context (of experience, age, job title, etc). They should not, on the other hand, be so finely drawn that players have no room to put their own interpretation on the role. The characteristics described, plus opinions and actions suggested, provide the player with a basis for the role.

To make the role play have some life, and to provide the opportunity for it to last longer than a couple of minutes, there needs to be an element of difference in the opinion or objectives of the two roles. Differences in character, weaknesses and blind spots can be sketched into the roles to highlight particular problems.

The allocation of male and female roles can be a problem. Ideally, all roles should be equally applicable to both sexes. This can lead to some very clumsy language so it is worth making the point that 'he' could just as easily be 'she' and vice versa. If you use names this transferability becomes more difficult although there are a few sexually neutral names (like Pat, Chris and Jo) but this still leaves the problem of he or she or, worse, s/he and his/her. There are, of course, occasions on which it is desirable for a woman to play the part of a man, and the other way about, in which case names and the sex of the player are no longer a problem in that way.

It is possible to use fun names such as B. Keen, Bodgett & Scarper (Builders) or suchlike; their acceptability will depend on the group and are best used sparingly. Use simple, straightforward language and try to keep the briefing as short as possible. Time spent absorbing the information is not, in itself, very productive. However, in more complex situations it is sometimes essential to provide a realistic amount of information in order to give the scene some depth and scope for the development of options, alternative solutions and a range of outcomes.

The business of writing your own role plays is time consuming but very rewarding if you can 'hook' the interest and imagination of the group with a situation with which they can identify easily; their enthusiasm is enhanced and the learning greater. Review sessions under these circumstances can be more difficult, however, as one struggles to separate what happened in the role play from reality in order to concentrate on the effects of the participants' behaviour.

Checklist: Writing role plays

1. Choose a situation (industry, environment, problem) with which you are familiar.
2. Consider carefully what lessons you wish to draw and construct the characters and situations accordingly.
3. Keep the language simple and appropriate to your audience.
4. Do not tie down the players so tightly that there is no room to improvise, to react to what is said or done, or to interpret events in different ways.
5. Keep briefing as short as you can but give enough detail of the characters to make them recognizable, credible and with some depth in a given context of position, age, etc.
6. Always try to build in a difference - of opinion, of character, of attitude, etc - to enliven the play and make the players confront the problems described.
7. Try to avoid confusion over male and female roles and be careful with the awkward language associated with that problem (s/he, his/hers/ their, him/her/them). Take care with names.

PART 2

ROLE PLAY ACTIVITIES

Chapter 4:

Negotiation role plays

We all have to negotiate from time to time. We may, for example, be buying a car, setting a time for a teenager to be home or trying to settle a dispute with a retailer or supplier. At work we may be negotiating a wage settlement, buying raw materials or reaching agreement with our peers about the sharing of resources. Negotiation is about getting a good deal. It is also, usually, about keeping an existing relationship alive to negotiate again in the future. The seller wants the customer to come back, the manager does not want to arouse a sense of grievance by driving too hard a bargain with his staff.

Negotiation is often conducted as positional bargaining, where both sides fight from prepared ramparts and feel reluctant to climb down over anything. Conflict arises easily in these circumstances. It is possible to adopt a more principled approach by producing creative solutions for mutual gain. This can result in a win-win situation in which each side has satisfied some or all of its major interests.

The skills required for successful negotiation include:

- assertiveness;
- inventing creative options;
- dealing with emotion and conflict;
- gaining agreement and commitment;

- discovering interests and common ground;
- establishing facts;
- removal of personal issues;
- win-win solutions;
- questioning skills;
- listening effectively (including summarizing and reflecting);
- understanding body language;
- establishing rapport;
- observation, interpretation and judgement;
- influencing skills.

All these skills need practice. Role playing can provide the opportunity for participants to practise and rehearse different skills and approaches in a supportive environment. The following scenarios will raise some or all of these issues.

THE BUILDING SITE
Role Play 1

Time guide Up to 3 hours, including 45 minutes for preparation and 40 minutes for review.

Participants 5 plus observers.

Equipment Desk, chairs and tables.(Trainers may wish to provide a choice of formal or informal seating for participants to choose their own preferred setting.)

Copies of the two general briefs for the two sides and appropriate brief for each participant. Copies of everything for the observers.

Notes for role players (Handout 4, page 48) if required. Observers' checklists (for an example see Handout 3, page 47).

Flipchart or whiteboard to record points from the debrief.

Video camera, tripod, recorder and TV monitor (if required).

LEARNING POINTS AND SKILLS PRACTISED

- All the general negotiation skills which include questioning, listening, proposing, bargaining and observation of non-verbal signals.
- Identification of the other side's interests and objectives.
- Defining negotiating strategies and objectives.
- Suggesting creative options.
- Gaining agreement and commitment.
- The resolution of conflict and dealing with emotion.
- The importance of reaching mutually advantageous solutions.
- Negotiating as a representative of a group.

Procedure See notes on the procedure for conducting a role play (Checklist, page 49). Brief the group on the overall scenario and the lessons to be learnt. Allow 45 minutes for players to prepare. For this complex situation, the two sides will need to establish not only individual roles but also a group approach to the negotiation. Meanwhile, brief observers and set up the room to represent the building company's offices. Play may then proceed for some time (up to 1½ hours). At the end allow time for players to come out of role and go on to the review phase.

Review See notes on feedback and review in Chapter 2 (Handouts 1 & 2, pages 45 and 46).

In particular, the group should try to answer the following questions as part of the review.

- How well prepared were the 2 sides? Were their best and worst positions defined? Was their plan clear?
- Did the negotiation go according to plan?
- Was the common ground explored?
- Were the interests and objectives of the other side discovered or disclosed?
- Was the final outcome satisfactory for all?
- Did the residents effectively represent all their neighbours?
- How well did the participants propose, bargain and progress?

HANDOUT
Negotiation – the building site

General information for residents

Until 6 weeks ago, Sycamore Drive was a quiet cul-de-sac backing on to woodland on one side and the rear of the houses along the main road on the other. There is a wide mixture of houses; there are a few bungalows owned by older people, some semis occupied by younger families with children and there are a few bigger detached houses as well as a block of town or terraced houses. The residents are a mixture of people, there are a few professional people in the larger houses but the majority are middle class working people and there are a few retired couples. There are about 100 people living in the Drive of whom about 25 are children under 14.

Six weeks ago a construction site was opened at the end of the Drive. Planning permission was granted 3 months ago to Empire Food Halls Ltd to develop 14 acres of the woodland for the erection of one of their supermarkets including car parking and a filling station. This planning application and its granting were not well publicized, although both Council and company did do the legal minimum in this respect. The residents were all taken by surprise when the work started. The construction company has circulated leaflets apologizing for any temporary disturbance and asking to be informed of any problems but no one has been able to get hold of anyone in authority at the company. Complaints to the police and local authority have been equally ineffective, both organizations claiming only very limited powers to do anything to help.

The noise, dust, litter and in particular the extra traffic arising from the construction work are becoming unbearable. Lorries carrying cement etc have been using the Drive as the only access to the site. There is no pavement in the Drive and pedestrians have to walk in the road: this is aggravated by the number of construction workers' cars parked in the Drive. The drivers of the heavy lorries are reckless and drive at speeds up to 40 mph and children in particular are at risk. There have been several near misses and it is felt that it is only a matter of time before there is an accident. Before the site opened the Drive was used by all the local children to play in. This is now impossible and potentially lethal. Several residents work night shifts and the increased traffic and noise has upset them immensely. At least one resident complains of cracks appearing in his house, an occurrence he blames on the heavy traffic. The language and inconsiderate behaviour of the workmen also give rise to concern. A further major complaint is over the level of security at the site. It is unfenced, unlit and virtually unattended outside working hours. This is seen as a real cause of concern, in particular for the safety of children who may stray on to the site. Building sites are inherently dangerous places, and one local child has already fallen into a large pit, fortunately without injury.

After a particularly close near miss on the road between a lorry and a resident's 8-year-old son on his way to school yesterday, there was a residents meeting attended by nearly all the adults. It was a stormy meeting raising many issues. All the aggravation and concern over the effects of the construction work came out as did concern for longer-term issues like increased traffic once the supermarket is open, the effects on property prices in the area and the numbers of heavy lorries delivering to the site as well as the necessity of creating another access to avoid Sycamore Drive altogether. A proposal to block the road until someone from the company came to put things right was narrowly defeated. A small residents' committee was elected and tasked with gaining some improvement in the situation.

This committee consists of a recently retired executive, a shift worker with a 12-year-old son, and a mother of 3 young children, who has an office service business running from home. Finally, this morning, a meeting has been arranged between the three members of the residents' committee and the development manager of Empire.

Empire is a well known local company and has been in business for many years. Its reputation has been high for quality, although there was a scandal a few years ago over the development of one of their earlier stores.

HANDOUT
Negotiation – the building site

Brief for the development manager and contractor

You are the development manager of Empire Food Halls Ltd. You have recently acquired 14 acres of land at the end of Sycamore Drive and gained planning permission for the erection of a new super-market with car parking and a filling station. The construction work started 6 weeks ago and you are very pleased with the progress of the development. The contractors who are building the store have really got a move on and you may be finished a little ahead of schedule if they continue at this rate. Your brother-in-law manages the site for the contractors and you and he act as the link between the company and the contractors.

You have both agreed to meet a committee from the residents of Sycamore Drive after the chairman's secretary informed you that they wished to talk to you about traffic and site security. She has arranged the meeting and you have not spoken directly to anyone from the Committee.

This development is critical to the company. You have invested a great deal of money in the land and have borrowed heavily to finance the construction. The sooner the building is finished the sooner you can start to trade on the site and the less interest you have to pay. Your contractors are subject to heavy penalty clauses if they fail to complete on time and there are incentives built into the contracts to encourage an early completion. The store must be finished as soon as possible. From the point of view of both you and your brother-in-law's firm the financial viability of the project rests in speed of completion, the absolute elimination of waste, and complete control of costs. There is not much margin for error or contingency and the costing has been worked out in great detail.

The successful completion of this project, however, could influence your ability to expand further in competition with the large national chains.

The planning permission was granted surprisingly quickly and you suspect that your chairman has had a significant influence on the planning committee to get such a quick decision. You were a little disturbed by the speed with which all the formalities were handled. You made sure that all the legal requirements of notification and approval were met. You were surprised not to hear anything from the local residents and you suspect that they were unaware of the proposed development until it was too late. The land you are building on belonged to your chairman's mother who retains a stake in the project and lives nearby. Her land backs on to the new site and occupies all the road frontage through which a new access would have to be made if you wanted another. The chairman tells you that she and he are very unwilling to forego any more land for the development. All this makes you a little uneasy, but you are sure you are fireproof on everything, legally speaking.

You do not know what the residents' committee wants to talk about other than it has something to do with traffic and site security.

You are not concerned about site security at this stage; until later in the building programme there is little worth stealing and this is a problem for the contractors. The construction traffic may be a problem for the residents. They might have a point there, but you are more concerned about the building programme; time and speed are critical. The contractors have already dismissed one materials supplier for failure to deliver on time. There is a security visit programme arranged with a local security firm for the hours of darkness and weekends.

The contractors' performance so far has exceeded all expectations and on the occasional visit that you or the chairman have paid to the site you have been struck by the sense of urgency, the bustle and the level of sheer hard work that is going on. In particular the delivery programme seems to be excellent; vehicles are in, unloaded and away in a very quick time.

In a few weeks' time you will have to ensure that the site is fenced as more attractive equipment and materials are delivered to site. Currently the groundwork contractors are approaching completion of the footings, drains, roadways and pipe work. The steel erectors are beginning to work on the building frameworks.

You are quite happy to give any reassurance to the residents about the length of time the building, and therefore the extra traffic, will last and about the effect the new development will eventually have upon their property values and the general environment. After all, this development is an attractive one and residents will benefit, too, from the proximity of a high quality food store nearby. Overall you are sure that, whatever the locals' concerns, you can keep things on an even keel and satisfy any complaints. Your construction programme is under way, seems to be working to plan and you cannot afford to change it in any significant way. Indeed, your plans include an intention to move to working at weekends once the ground and steelwork is complete in three weeks' time so the pace of work will increase. From the residents' point of view this can only reduce the period of time that any slight inconvenience may last.

HANDOUT
Negotiation – the building site

Brief for the retired executive

You have lived in Sycamore Drive for 5 years. You moved here 3 years before you retired because it was quiet, a pleasant neighbourhood and there was little traffic. You accept that there has to be progress and have no real objection in principle to the new development. You are concerned, however, that as the owner of the last bungalow before the boundary of the site you will be overlooked by the new site and privacy is important to you. You want to know what arrangements for landscaping and maintaining your privacy, in particular, are being made. In fact it was this concern that led you to volunteer for the committee in the first place. You have tried to talk to someone at Empire several times but have never had a satisfactory response. Several letters have also never received an answer.

In the meanwhile, the noise, traffic and mess is a real nuisance and you want to take the firm to task for the conduct of their workmen who seem to have no respect for your property; litter is for ever being thrown over the hedge and you are sure that some of them are using it as a toilet, even though 'portaloos' are available on the site. Future traffic levels, when the site is finished, also concern you.

The previous occupants of your house added an extension over the garage and the very useful room that it created was one of the reasons for your buying the property. Now, because of the constant passage of heavy traffic, the walls are beginning to crack and the garage looks as if it is subsiding. It is difficult to prove but there were no cracks 6 weeks ago.

HANDOUT
Negotiation – the building site

Brief for the shift worker

You have lived in Sycamore Drive for the last 10 years and you moved here when your 12-year-old son was a baby. For the last 4 years you have worked at the local power station as charge engineer for the night shift. Your normal routine during the week has been totally disrupted by the noise from the building site and the traffic. You have rarely slept properly and you have had to catch up with your sleep at weekends when things are quieter. This has done no good for your relationship with your wife, who works during the week and is now upset that you never see her or your son except as you come home in the morning.

That would be bad enough but last week your son and a friend wandered into the building site and your son fell into an excavation some 15ft deep as the side collapsed under his weight. Fortunately, he was able to crawl out up the slope created by the fall of earth. He was frightened and filthy when he got home but extremely lucky to have escaped burial. You had a look at the site and are horrified that there is complete freedom of access. Almost anything could happen in there. You are not sure but you think that there is a legal obligation upon the contractor to make the site safe. Your election to this committee gives you the chance to make your point to Empire and to try to force them to do something about the safety problem. There are a lot of children in the road and you do not want to see an accident from one of these speeding lorries. The problem of future traffic levels also worries you and you want to insist upon a new access to reduce the pressure on Sycamore Drive.

HANDOUT
Negotiation – the building site

Brief for the businesswoman working from home

You have lived in Sycamore Drive for the last 3 years. For the last year your husband has been on a contract in Saudi Arabia and you are left with 3 children aged 4, 6 and 9. Your business, which you conduct from home, is to provide a clerical, secretarial and office service for small businesses locally. This occupies a great deal of your time and you have to leave the children to their own devices for a lot of the day when they are not at school. Your youngest goes to a nursery school in the mornings and you have arranged for a neighbour to look after him most afternoons with her own child of much the same age. You are frightened out of your wits by the thought of the accident that you feel is bound to happen soon to some child going to or from school on the Drive. These great lorries dash up and down between all the parked cars, making it really dangerous.

You are so worried you have agreed to form part of this residents' committee to try and get the lorries stopped or at least get them to slow down. You were all for barricading the road but were eventually persuaded to wait and try to convince the company to do something about it. You have tried to talk to the boss of Empire before but were fobbed off by some snooty woman in the office.

If you do not get some satisfactory answers you are determined to block the road somehow. Maybe some cars awkwardly parked at intervals down the road will slow them down. You want to insist that the company open another access to the site to prevent traffic using Sycamore Drive as much as possible.

THE YOUTH CLUB

Role Play 2

Time guide Up to 2 hours, including 40 minutes for preparation and review.

Participants 3 plus observers.

Equipment Desk, chairs and tables.(Trainers may wish to provide a choice of formal or informal seating for participants to choose their own preferred setting.)

Copies of the general information for all. Copies of the appropriate briefs for each participant. Copies of everything for the observers.

Notes for role players (Handout 4, page 48) if required. Observers' checklists (for an example see Handout 3, page 47).

Flipchart or whiteboard to record points during the debrief.

Video camera, tripod, recorder and TV monitor (if required).

LEARNING POINTS AND SKILLS PRACTISED

- All the general negotiation skills which include questioning, listening, proposing, bargaining and observation of non-verbal signals.
- Identification of the other side's interests and objectives.
- Defining negotiating strategies and objectives.
- Suggesting creative options.
- The handling and resolution of conflict and dealing with emotion.
- The importance of reaching mutually advantageous solutions.

Procedure See notes on conducting a role play (Checklist, page 49). Brief participants and allow 40 minutes for preparation. This is a complex situation and the local residents will need to absorb their individual roles and agree a joint approach. Meanwhile brief observers and lay out the room to represent the youth club leader's office. Allow play to continue for up to 40 minutes before allowing players to come out of role and start the review.

Review See notes on feedback and review in Chapter 2 (Handouts 1 & 2, pages 45 and 46).

In particular, the group should try to answer the following questions as part of the review.

- How well prepared were the two sides?
- Was the common ground explored?
- Was the final outcome satisfactory for all? If not, why not?
- How well did the participants propose, bargain and progress?
- How well were the interests and requirements of the two sides explored?
- Were the final arrangements clear to all?

HANDOUT
Negotiation – the youth club

General information for all

The Riverside Youth Club has its premises in a converted warehouse down near the river. It exists to provide a place for the young people of the town to meet and to give them the opportunity to develop hobbies and interests in order to keep them off the streets and out of the pubs. It caters for teenagers between 14 and 18.

A range of activities are available in the centre including sports – badminton, basketball, pool, etc – repair facilities for cycles and motor bikes, gymnasium equipment and some good disco equipment. All these facilities have been provided over time by local businesses and by self help. There is one full time leader paid by the local authority who give the club a small grant each year as well. In fact the club has had a remarkably successful existence, due largely to the enthusiasm of the first leader who gave it up a few months ago through ill health.

The attendance at the centre is very high and most nights see anything up to 60 club members gathered at the centre.

Last night a group of half-a-dozen youths ran up the lane at the back of the club, breaking windows, kicking holes in fences, upsetting dustbins and finally setting fire to a wooden garage, fortunately with no car inside, at the bottom of the yard of the end house. This was late at night and caused distress to several elderly residents who were woken up and were very frightened.

A meeting has been arranged in the leader's office between the youth club leader and some local residents.

HANDOUT
Negotiation – the youth club

Brief for the youth club leader

You have been in charge of the club for about 3 months now and you have done your best to keep up the standards set by your very able predecessor. In fact, you are very pleased that, if anything, the level of attendance has gone up since your arrival. You have noticed, however, that there is a tendency for a rowdy element to come in from time to time. You feel their presence is disruptive and could spoil the reputation that the club has gained in the community.

Last night a group of lads, who had been drinking, came into the club causing a stir, started a minor fight, broke a table and smashed some crockery before you managed to persuade them to leave. They were in an angry mood. You are fairly certain that these were the ones who caused the damage which the police told you about this morning. A call from a neighbour, Ted Oldham, asking for a meeting with you and another resident about last night makes you think that they too believe that the vandals came from the club. In fact you had never seen these particular lads before and you have given the police all the help you can in their search for them, although they are not very hopeful about identifying them or of catching them.

You are very proud of the record of the club and, only this morning, the police told you that they felt that the club had been one of the main reasons for the low level of youth misdemeanour in the area. You are anxious that this should continue, not least for your own reputation following, as you do, someone who seems to have been an exceptional man.

You are currently talking to several local tradesmen with a view to arranging a series of activities in which youngsters can be given basic skills in vehicle mechanics, DIY etc. Your predecessor had run

© David Turner 1992, published by Kogan Page

some of these and they had proved very popular and you have had several young people asking if they could be restarted. You also believe some sort of outdoor, more adventurous, activities would be attractive. So far, a general builder, a motorcycle repair specialist and a computer man have agreed to help with the indoor activities. You had intended to talk to Ted Oldham about him giving assistance with the building of a kit car since you are told that he is the service manager for a local car dealer. It is he that wants to talk to you about last night's incidents, and you hope you can somehow broach this subject with him.

HANDOUT
Negotiation – the youth club

The brief for Ted Oldham, club neighbour

You are Ted Oldham and you have lived in Riverside Road, in the end house, for the last 20 years. You are the service manager for a local car agent. Last night, after you had gone to bed, you were woken by a lot of yelling and shouting in the lane at the back which runs between your house and the warehouse/club building. You could hear bangs and crashes farther down. As you came to your window to look out you saw flames licking up the side of your wooden garage which is at the bottom of your yard at the back of the house. Within moments it was well alight and, by the time you got there, there was no hope of saving it. You called the fire brigade and the police. Fortunately you had left the car at work last night because it was part way through a service and you got a lift home from a workmate. It was not a very elegant garage but it was useful and you kept quite a lot of odds and ends in there.

You didn't actually see anyone putting a match to the garage but you are sure that it must have been done deliberately, given all the noise and the other damage that your neighbours have told you about. The noise of the people had come up the lane from the club at the other end and you assume that they had come from there.

This morning you spoke to several of your neighbours, some of whom are quite elderly, and everyone you spoke to had had some problem. Fences had holes kicked in them, dustbins had been up-ended and 5 windows in different houses have been broken to your knowledge. Two or three of your older neighbours were very frightened by the noise and, in one case, by a brick coming through their bedroom window as they lay in bed.

One of the people you spoke to this morning was Andrea Wilkins, who had a window broken and her dustbin upset. She is very angry and agreed to come with you to see the new leader of the club. You rang the centre earlier and a meeting is arranged with you and Andrea at the centre shortly. You have never had any dealings with the club, nor any problems before. You know this leader is new and, as you understand it, the last leader was very well regarded. You will not tolerate any further incidents of this kind and you want to get some reparation for the damage caused to your and your neighbours' property.

HANDOUT
Negotiation – the youth club

The brief for Andrea Wilkins, club neighbour

You are Andrea Wilkins and you live in Riverside Road; your house backs on to a lane that runs between the houses and the warehouse building in which the club is housed.

You were watching television last night when you became aware of a lot of noise – singing, laughing and shouting – coming from the lane. As you looked out there were bangs and crashes and you heard dustbins going over and the sound of breaking glass. You turned off the light to get a better look and to avoid being seen yourself. You saw 5 or 6 young men running up and down the lane. There was some light from neighbouring upstairs windows and you watched as they kicked fences, threw things into the back yards and continued to make a lot of noise. At that moment one of them threw something at the house and a large pane of glass in your kitchen window shattered. You stopped watching and ran to ring the police to report what was happening. By the time they arrived some 10 minutes later the youths had gone, a shed up the road was burning brightly and people were emerging to see the damage.

Your kitchen is a mess. It had only recently been decorated and there were scores in the paintwork, scratches in the worktops and it took you until 2am to be certain you had cleared up all the glass. Your next door neighbours, both over 80, were in an awful state last night after a brick had come through their bedroom window while they were in bed. You spent some considerable time helping them to clear up and reassuring them before they would go back to bed to sleep. This morning, talking to Ted from up the road, you agreed to accompany him to talk to the new leader at the club. Like Ted, you think that these vandals can only have come from the club and you do not want this sort of thing to happen again. In fact, you are very angry about the whole affair.

Before you moved here a few months ago, you had been involved on a voluntary basis with a youth club in the area from which you came. You are very interested in helping young people, but you cannot cope with rowdyism or vandalism. You had intended to approach this club, so near to you, to see if you could help. You have a Mountain Leadership Certificate and you are the PE teacher at the nearby comprehensive school. This job keeps you pretty busy, but being single, there is no reason why you should not help other groups as well. But you cannot bear the thought of becoming involved with a rough lot and you are having second thoughts about approaching the leader. You have heard that the last, well respected, leader has gone and that there is now a new person there.

THE PACKAGING PURCHASE

Role Play 3

Time guide Up to 1½ hours, including 30 minutes for preparation and review.

Participants 2 plus observers.

Equipment Desk, chairs and tables. (Trainers may wish to provide a choice of formal or informal seating for participants to choose their own preferred setting.)

One copy of the buyer's and the supplier's briefs for the participants and enough copies of both for the observers.

Notes for role players (Handout 4, page 48) if required.
Observers' checklists (for an example see Handout 3, page 47).

Flipchart or whiteboard to record points from the debrief.

Video camera, tripod, recorder and TV monitor (if required).

LEARNING POINTS AND SKILLS PRACTISED

- All the general negotiation skills which include questioning, listening, proposing, bargaining and observation of non-verbal signals.
- Identification of the other side's interests and objectives.
- Defining negotiating strategies and objectives.
- Suggesting creative options.
- Gaining agreement and commitment to mutually advantageous solutions.
- The importance of service and other factors as well as price.

Procedure See notes on conducting a role play (Checklist, page 49). Brief participants and allow ½ hour for preparation. Meanwhile brief observers and arrange furniture to represent the buyer's office. Allow play to continue for up to 30 minutes before allowing players to come out of role and start the review.

Review See notes on feedback and review in Chapter 2 (Handouts 1 & 2, pages 45 and 46).

In particular, the group should try to answer the following questions as part of the review.

- How well prepared were the two sides? Had they established best case and worst acceptable positions?
- Was the common ground explored?
- Was the final outcome satisfactory for all?
- How far were issues other than price brought in?
- How well did the participants propose, bargain and progress?

HANDOUT
Negotiation – the packaging purchase

Brief for the buyer

Your company produces a range of giftware that is sold through retail outlets nationwide. One of your major concerns is that the packaging should project the image of quality and accurately reflect the nature of the goods inside. Obviously, if the goods are used as gifts then the presentation of the packaging is very important.

You have bought your boxes for one line from the same supplier for the last 4 years. They have managed to produce good quality boxes, well printed to your specification and artwork, by the dates that you required them. They won the business each year by quoting a competitive rate and agreeing to the service that you required.

This year, like last, you require a total of 20,000 of these boxes, spread through the year, 3000 in January, 3000 in March, 5000 in June and the remainder in September. In addition this year, you would like an option to take up to a further 3000 at short notice if demand increases. The artwork this year will remain the same.

Last year you negotiated a price of 26p per box (compared with 28p the previous year). This was achieved by rescheduling delivery requirements and because other suppliers had put in very competitive quotes. In addition, last year's order was an increase of 25 per cent in volume over the previous year.

You have had two quotes from different suppliers for 33p/box for the quantities you require and you know that, in general, prices are likely to have to rise between 8 and 10 per cent this year. You would like to buy at no more than 30p for the same quantity and service as last year, but would like to get a better deal if possible.

In order to reduce the price there are some things you could offer. Although your storage facilities are limited, you could take in larger deliveries. If the price were right, you might be prepared to commit yourself to a deal on more than one year's supply. The normal deal has been payment within 90 days of deliveries, you might be prepared to reduce this to 30 days, again for the right deal.

You are anxious to finalize the arrangements for this year's supply of this line and you have arranged for the rep to see you later today to discuss it. Given their previous record on quality and service, this supplier is your preferred option: but you must still get the best deal you can.

HANDOUT
Negotiation – the packaging purchase

Brief for the supplier's representative

You have an appointment to see the buyer from one of your larger customers later today to talk about the contract for the supply of some packaging. You have provided this item for them for the last 4 years and, so far as you know, there have been no problems and they have always been happy with the quality and the service.

The item in question is a decorative box for one of their giftware lines that is sold nationally. They have given you the specification and the artwork, which you have already established will remain the same this year. You now, unknown to them, produce a similar box, using different artwork of course, for one of their competitors. But this makes little difference to the production costs.

Last year they ordered 20,000 in 4 spaced deliveries through the year. These you produced in one run and delivered to schedule from store. This is quite convenient for you, although it would help if you could deliver in one load when the printing, etc, is complete.

The price last year was a problem. This customer put you under a lot of pressure to retain the order against some stiff competition. They are a well-known firm and having them as a customer is good for your own image and credibility. To retain the order you quoted 26p per box but you have made no profit on the order as a result, and you were only able to go at that price after you had spoken to your boss for approval. The reasons it was agreed were that the volume was 25 per cent up on the previous year, and they agreed to take the boxes in 4 deliveries instead of 12 monthly ones.

This year you have to do a bit better. Board, printing and manufacturing costs have increased by 8 per cent and to break even you need to get something over 29p per box. You really need to improve on that and you hope to get 32 to 33p/box. Your competitors would probably be able to match a price of 33p. If you could reduce the number of deliveries, increase the overall volume or get an agreement to reduce the current credit terms of 90 days you might be able to make a profit at a lower figure than your best price of 33p.

It is worth remembering that the other customer who takes a similar pattern box has already agreed to pay 35p each.

RENTING FACTORY SPACE

Role Play 4

Time guide Up to 1¼ hours, including 25 minutes for preparation and review.

Participants 2 plus observers.

Equipment Desk, chairs and tables. (Trainers may wish to provide a choice of formal or informal seating for participants to choose their own preferred setting.)

A copy of the appropriate brief for each participant, and enough copies of both for the observers.

Notes for role players (Handout 4, page 48) if required. Observers' checklists (for an example see Handout 3, page 47).

Flipchart or whiteboard to record points from the debrief.

Video camera, tripod, recorder and TV monitor (if required).

LEARNING POINTS AND SKILLS PRACTISED

- All the general negotiation skills which include questioning, listening, proposing, bargaining and observation of non-verbal signals.
- Identification of the other side's interests and objectives.
- Defining negotiating strategies and objectives.
- Suggesting creative options.
- Gaining agreement and commitment to mutually advantageous solutions.
- The importance of other factors as well as price.

Procedure See notes on conducting a role play (Checklist, page 49). Brief the participants and allow 25 minutes for preparation. Meanwhile brief the observers and arrange the room to represent the office of the Agent. Allow play to continue for up to 30 minutes before giving players a little time to come out of role and start the review.

Review See notes on feedback and review in Chapter 2 (Handouts 1 & 2, pages 45 and 46).

In particular, the group should try to answer the following questions as part of the review.

- How well were the participants prepared? Were their objectives and strategies clear at the outset?
- How far were factors other than price an issue?
- Was the final outcome satisfactory to all?
- Were the interests and requirements of the two sides fully explored?
- How well did the two sides propose, bargain and progress?

HANDOUT
Negotiation – renting factory space

Brief for the agent for the owner of the space

You represent the owner of a small estate of industrial units of mixed sizes. These range from 20,000 sq ft to 5,000 sq ft. You are responsible for the management of the estate.

At present you have one unit of 7,000 sq ft available, one end unit of 10,000 and another end unit of 12,000. The 2 smaller ones are adjacent and could be rented out as one unit.

All the units are about 16 years old and beginning to look a little tired although structurally they are all sound. You have taken care to ensure that the maintenance of the fabric and the services has been carried out regularly. All units have space heating, a little office space, 3-phase electricity supply and a good standard of lighting.

Access to all the units is good and anything up to 40ft lorries can use the estate roads, and doorways in the units are large enough to take fork-lift truck traffic. Each end unit has a large concrete apron to the side as well as at the front as every other unit has. The estate is well signposted and local roads are good.

Rents on the other units range from £4 per sq ft per year to £6 per sq ft per year. You are being increasingly troubled by the cost of maintenance and you would like to get at least £6 per sq ft for these units. You like to arrange a lease that is renewable annually.

Because of the location and the nature of business of some of the other tenants you wish to impose various conditions upon any new tenant. You want there to be no Sunday working. No suitable drainage is available for anything other than domestic or similar liquid waste, so chemical waste must be the tenant's responsibility.

You are keen to keep the estate looking as clean as possible and, therefore, you want no operations that will spill out on to the roads. You are very particular about cleanliness and housekeeping on tenants' units must be of a high standard. Rubbish, broken pallets and discarded equipment must not be left lying around. You try and insert a clause in the contract allowing you to arrange for clearing unsightly materials and pass the charge to the tenant. You operate a contract with a local waste collector who undertakes to clear any full waste container within 4 hours on working days. You charge this out at an annual rate of 15p per sq ft of space occupied.

A security service is available but it costs you £25 per week per unit for security checks and patrols through the quiet hours. This service you would wish to charge out to any new tenant.

The local council business rates on each unit are payable by the tenant. Currently they amount to 50p per sq ft per year.

You have had a call from a prospective tenant and you are due to meet shortly in your office.

HANDOUT
Negotiation – renting factory space

Brief for the prospective tenant

You are the proprietor of a small fruit and vegetable wholesale business that currently operates out of an old warehouse near the docks. This site gives you 9000 sq ft of space which is insufficient for your needs now that you have acquired the contract to provide fresh vegetables for the victualling of Royal Navy ships. This represents a large increase in volume for you and is a prestigious contract. Your very scruffy premises are no longer suitable.

You need new premises of at least 13,000 sq ft and would pay for more if the price were right. Your current rental is £2.50 per sq ft per year. You know that you will have to pay more but profit margins are tight and you cannot afford to pay more than £5 per sq ft. If you can get it for less you would like to do so. In fact, any deal that postponed extra costs would be beneficial, so the terms of payment of rent, the negotiation of rent increases and other sundry associated expenses are critical. The most important thing is to keep the rent and local council rates bill down. If you have to shoulder some other costs under your control, which can be phased, reduced or put off, that would be better than paying a higher rental or associated charge.

You are in a hurry to move. The Navy contract starts in one month and you would like to be installed in the new premises by then. You need good lighting, since much of your work is done in the early hours of the morning and you need a 3-phase electricity supply for the charging of your 3 fork-lift trucks and the operation of the conveyor belts on your pre-packing line. You must have access for 40ft trailers both for end loading and side loading. Your own vans, 6 of them, need parking space.

You have seen a small estate with vacant units. It looks clean but the units themselves look a bit rough. Perhaps you can get a good price for one of these and smarten it up a bit yourself later when the Navy contract starts to pay off. You have arranged to see the Agent for the estate shortly in his office.

SHARING EQUIPMENT
Role Play 5

Time guide Up to $1\frac{1}{4}$ hours, including 20 minutes for preparation and 20 minutes for review.

Participants 2 plus observers.

Equipment Desk, chairs and tables. (Trainers may wish to provide a choice of formal or informal seating for participants to choose their own preferred setting.)

One copy of the appropriate brief for each participant, and enough copies of both for the observers.

Notes for role players (Handout 4, page 48) if required.
Observers' checklists (for an example see Handout 3, page 47).

Flipchart or whiteboard to record points from the debrief.

Video camera, tripod, recorder and TV monitor (if required).

LEARNING POINTS AND SKILLS PRACTISED

- All the general negotiation skills which include questioning, listening, proposing, bargaining and observation of non-verbal signals.
- Identification of the other side's interests and objectives.
- Defining negotiating strategies and objectives.
- Suggesting creative options.
- Gaining agreement and commitment to mutually advantageous solutions.

Procedure See notes on conducting a role play (Checklist, page 49). Brief participants and allow 20 minutes for preparation. Meanwhile, brief observers and arrange the room to represent a room at the garage owner's house. Allow play to continue for up to 30 minutes before giving players a little time to come out of role and start the review.

Review See notes on feedback and review in Chapter 2 (Handouts 1 & 2, pages 45 and 46).

In particular, the group should try to answer the following questions as part of the review.

- How well were the participants prepared? Were their objectives and strategies clear at the outset?
- Was the final outcome satisfactory to both sides?
- Were the interests and requirements of the two sides fully explored? Were all the factors considered?
- How well did the two sides propose, bargain and progress?

HANDOUT
Negotiation – sharing equipment

Brief for the kit car builder

You run a small business from a workshop alongside your home. You advertise your services to the general public, offering to acquire and build any kit car for them. You will either buy the kit from the supplier and build it or rescue half-built models or build from scratch kits bought by a client.

Business is good and there has been a lot of interest in your services. You are considering building cars on spec to sell, and you are considering taking on another person to help you. What you are short of is sophisticated equipment. Most of the models you are currently handling and those you are considering building for yourself to sell are sporty jobs which need careful and accurate tuning. At present you have to go on bended knee to a couple of local garages to hire their equipment when it is free. This is expensive and inconvenient. You are often held up, waiting, sometimes for days, to use their equipment. Somehow you want to have free access to good testing and tuning equipment.

This equipment, for which there are several suppliers, is very expensive. Even the basic models with few extras cost in the order of £20,000. The cost for the all-singing, all-dancing models can be as high as £50,000.

For your needs the basic model would suffice. You wish to approach the second-hand car-dealer next door who has a small workshop to see if you can arrange to acquire the equipment on a joint basis. Your neighbour already has a very old set of equipment which is used regularly. There is a full-time fitter who complains constantly about its unreliability.

You need the equipment for about 1 to 1½ days per week (in 2-hour sessions approx). Ideally you would like it to be situated on your premises but it would not hurt if it were next door. The most you can afford is £7,500 and £2,000 of that would be a bank loan. If you went, jointly, for a basic machine your neighbour's contribution would have to be between £12,500 and £14,500.

You would like unrestricted access at any time to the equipment and are quite happy to come to some deal about insurance, maintenance and even power supply providing it is equitable. There would need to be some agreement on training as well.

You have mentioned your idea to your neighbour and some interest was expressed. You have arranged to meet at his house in a few minutes to discuss the proposition.

HANDOUT
Negotiation – sharing equipment

Brief for the second-hand car-dealer

You have a second-hand car business. You employ a full-time fitter who ensures that all your cars are mechanically sound before sale and who also services and repairs cars you have sold where customers have paid for extended guarantees. There is a small amount of maintenance business from the general public too.

Your garage is not particularly well equipped and, in particular, is lacking reliable, modern testing and tuning equipment. This equipment is expensive (about £20,000 for the cheapest, simplest models up to about £50,000 for more complex and comprehensive equipment) and you cannot afford that sort of money. If you had some decent equipment you might be able to get some Ministry of Transport testing work (MOT). In practice a basic model would suffice, but it would be nice to get as good a set of equipment as possible.

Your current equipment is about 25 years old and will have little or no trade-in value. It is pretty unreliable and your fitter is always complaining about it.

Your neighbour, who runs a kit car assembly business from home next door, mentioned to you the other day a need for access to some testing and tuning equipment and perhaps the two of you should buy one jointly. This struck you as quite a good idea and you are meeting shortly in your house to discuss the idea in more detail.

You cannot afford more than £12,000 without recourse to borrowing, which you are reluctant to do. In the last resort you could probably just about afford to borrow a further £2000 from your bank. You would really only be prepared to borrow for a better than basic machine. You have done some digging around to see if there are any reconditioned or second-hand sets around. They are, apparently, very few and far between and much sought after. You considered leasing and none of the suppliers were interested in a leasing deal, except on the most expensive models. As far as you can tell, credit deals, with payment spread over several months, would be unlikely to be forthcoming – but perhaps if you pushed hard enough . . .

You would need fairly constant access to the equipment, particularly if you became a licensed testing station. Both you and your fitter would need training and because of the anticipated usage that you foresee, you must have the equipment on your premises. On insurance, maintenance and calibration (essential if you want MOT work) you would like the minimum possible cost. You have to keep your overheads to a minimum.

In short, you are really quite keen to get a deal, since you can see that you might have control over some new equipment at a much reduced cost and have the opportunity to go for more, and more lucrative, business in the form of MOT work.

MAINTENANCE OR PRODUCTION?

Role Play 6

Time guide Up to 1½ hours, including 30 minutes for preparation and 30 minutes for review.

Participants 2 plus observers.

Equipment Desk, chairs and tables. (Trainers may wish to provide a choice of formal or informal seating for participants to choose their own preferred setting.)

One copy of the appropriate brief for each participant, and enough copies of both for the observers.

Notes for role players (Handout 4, page 48) if required. Observers' checklists (for an example see Handout 3, page 47).

Flipchart or whiteboard to record points from the debrief.

Video camera, tripod, recorder and TV monitor (if required).

LEARNING POINTS AND SKILLS PRACTISED

- All the general negotiation skills which include questioning, listening, proposing, bargaining and observation of non-verbal signals.
- Identification of common interests and objectives.
- Suggesting creative options.
- Gaining agreement and commitment to mutually advantageous solutions.

Procedure See notes on conducting a role play (Checklist, page 49). Brief the participants, allow 30 minutes for preparation. Meanwhile brief the observers and arrange the room to represent the manager's office. Allow play to continue for up to 30 minutes, before giving players a little time to come out of role and start the review.

Review See notes on feedback and review in Chapter 2 (Handouts 1 & 2, pages 45 and 46).

In particular, the group should try to answer the following questions as part of the review.

- How well were the participants prepared? Were their objectives clear?
- Was the final outcome satisfactory to both sides and the company?
- Were the interests and requirements of the two sides fully explored? Were all the factors considered?
- How well did the two sides propose and bargain?

HANDOUT
Negotiation – maintenance or production?

General brief for all

Haulover Transport and Distribution plc lease a warehouse for their central storage function. It has been in residence for the last 7 years and handles over 20,000 cases per day, loads some 35 vehicles daily and can store up to 15,000 pallets in a narrow-aisle, high-bay warehouse. This gives very intensive use of space, both horizontally and vertically, and reduces movement space to a minimum.

The lease stipulates that the building shall be redecorated at regular intervals by the lessee. It requires the outside to be done at 5-year intervals and the inside every 7 years. It is now time for the internal decoration to be done. The programme for this work is the responsibility of the manager of the property department at head office who must agree this programme with the distribution manager at the warehouse in order to minimize the disruption. It is now February and the work must be done by December. There is a budget of £15,000 for this contract. Some of that money may well be bid for by Distribution if their staff are used to prepare the work round the contractors (for instance moving stock for access during painting or to avoid splash damage). There is shortly to be a meeting in the distribution manager's office to agree a timetable for the work.

HANDOUT
Negotiation – maintenance or production?

Brief for the property department manager

You are responsible for fulfilling the terms of the lease on the warehouse. This includes the internal redecoration. You must arrange with the distribution manager the most suitable programme for that redecoration bearing in mind your budget of £15,000 and the need to minimize disruption to the warehouse operation. You are keen to come in under budget because there are other jobs around for which you need extra cash.

Ideally the whole operation would be done during the day on weekdays to keep the cost down. You are also perfectly certain that this will be unacceptable.

Your quotes are as follows:

Roof and aerial steel work (incl hire of mobile scaffolding)	£5,500
Walls and partitions	£2,000
Offices	£1,500

These prices will double for weekend work and treble for night work. These prices are based on a standard rate per square metre. So if, for instance, half the roof were done at night and half during the day at weekends the cost would be £8250 + £5500 = £13,750 for the whole roof.

The prices are valid for 5 months and the contractor requires 2 weeks notice to start work. If the work is delayed beyond July the price is likely to increase. Work will be supervised by a visiting foreman, who will be available at the start of each working shift and on occasional visits. He will have a portable 'phone.

The time estimated by the contractor for doing the job will depend upon the number of gangs at work. He estimates, however, that one gang could reasonably complete one aisle per day for the roof and could do all the walls and partitions in two weeks. The offices will take one gang a further 7 working days. Two gangs working would halve the time for each job. Three is the maximum number of gangs he could supply at any one time.

The roof space of the warehouse proper covers 70 per cent racked storage space with 36 aisles, 25 per cent load assembly and packing areas and 5 per cent loading/unloading bays. The way that each of these sectors is handled is entirely a matter for negotiation.

You are due to meet the distribution manager shortly.

HANDOUT
Negotiation – maintenance or production?

Brief for the distribution manager

You are shortly due to meet the property department manager to arrange the details of the redecoration of the warehouse.

You are very keen to minimize the disruption to your operation and the ideal would be for all the work to be done at night or at weekends. Realistically, this is unlikely to be acceptable to the property department's budget for the task.

There are a few essentials that you wish to put across. First, the roof over the load assembly and packing areas cannot be tackled during the day; there is far too much traffic for it to be curtailed in any way. Equally, loads are stored there overnight for early morning despatch and could not readily be moved without risk of misdirecting goods. This area, therefore should be done on Saturdays, allowing your staff to restore order on overtime on the Sunday. There will be a cost to be borne for that operation – but only for a couple of people for 3 or 4 hours at double time (approx £15 per man-hour).

Second, you want no more than two aisles blocked by mobile scaffolding at any one time during the day. At night or at weekends there would be no restriction, and this is your preferred option. There will be a cost involved in extracting the stock required from the affected aisles the previous evening (approx 4 man-hours per night @ £8 per hour) if the work is to be done during the week by day.

Third, walls are not a problem, apart from the wall over and around the loading bays (15 per cent of the total wall area) which can properly only be done at night or at weekends (not Saturday morning).

The offices are not a major problem, but you will only want one gang in there at a time, and staff will be in the way. The contractor may, for ease of access, prefer to do the offices at the weekend.

Safety is of paramount importance, as are cleanliness and house-keeping. You will want to insist that the decorators clear up after them, obey the safety rules and are properly briefed on them (no exceptions; every contractor coming on site must be briefed on safety). You will want to reserve the right to remove any contractor who misbehaves or disregards the safety rules. A person who is in charge of the contractors is to be present at all times. Security will be charged at £100 for each night worked overseeing contractors and £75 per day at weekends.

NEIGHBOURLY EXCHANGE

Role Play 7

Time guide Up to 1 hour, including 15 minutes for preparation and 20 minutes for review.

Participants 2 plus observers.

Equipment Desk, chairs and tables. (Trainers may wish to provide a choice of formal or informal seating for participants to choose their own preferred setting.)

One copy of the appropriate brief for each participant, and enough copies of both for the observers.

Notes for role players (Handout 4, page 48) if required. Observers' checklists (for an example see Handout 3, page 47).

Flipchart or whiteboard to record points from the debrief.

Video camera, tripod, recorder and TV monitor (if required).

LEARNING POINTS AND SKILLS PRACTISED

- All the general negotiation skills which include questioning, listening, proposing, bargaining and observation of non-verbal signals.
- Identification of common interests and objectives.
- Suggesting creative options.
- Gaining agreement and commitment to mutually advantageous solutions.

Procedure See notes on conducting a role play (Checklist, page 49). Brief participants and allow 15 minutes for preparation. Meanwhile brief observers and arrange furniture to represent a room in the cabinet maker's house. Allow play to continue for up to 30 minutes before allowing players to come out of role and begin the review.

Review See notes on feedback and review in Chapter 2 (Handouts 1 & 2, pages 45 and 46).

In particular, the group should try to answer the following questions as part of the review.

- How well were the participants prepared? Were their objectives clear?
- Was the final outcome satisfactory to both sides?
- Were all the factors considered? Did all the possible options emerge?
- How well did the two sides propose and bargain?
- Did each side achieve greatest benefit at least cost to the other?

HANDOUT
Negotiation – neighbourly exchange

Brief for the cabinet maker

You live in a large house at the end of a street in which most of the houses have no access to the rear of their premises except through the house. Being on the end you have a driveway that leads into your rear garden and to the old 2-storey barn that you currently use as a garage, garden shed and, on the first floor, a children's rumpus room.

Your children are virtually grown up and you now wish to start your own cabinet making business using the barn as your workshop. You will only need about two-thirds of the space, so the existing bricked-off garage could remain. You have outline planning permission and you understand that final approval is only a matter of a rubber stamp.

A couple of days ago you met your immediate neighbour in the pub and you chatted about your ideas for the business. You explained that capital was a bit short for the alterations that needed to be made to the building and that the priority would have to be the woodworking machinery that you require. There was a limited amount of building work to be done but the barn needs completely new electrical wiring, separately metered, sufficient for the loading which the new machinery could impose. This neighbour is an electrician for the electricity company and expressed an interest in doing the work for you. You agreed to talk about it and he had a good look around and measured up a couple of days ago. This sounds as if it might be an inexpensive, or at least cheaper, way of doing it and you have arranged for him to come round and talk about it in a few minutes.

The most you can afford for the wiring is £1500 and you hope that it will cost significantly less than that if it is being done 'on the side' by your neighbour. Time is not a particular problem, although once you have the full planning permission you would like to have all the building work, rewiring, etc done within 2 months.

It seems a good deal for you to get your wiring cheaply and for him to have some extra income. You hope that after his look around he can give you some firm prices.

When you were talking to him he mentioned that he had a 1929 racing car and afterwards took you to see it. You were intensely jealous of him and would love to be able to drive it and to help bring it back to its pristine condition. That would be a real thrill.

HANDOUT
Negotiation – neighbourly exchange

Brief for the electrician

You are an electrician working for the local electricity company. You live in a row of houses with no access to the rear of the properties except through the house. Your neighbour is at the end and has a driveway to an old barn at the back. This is used as a combined garage and shed and playroom for the children.

Recently you met in the pub and got talking about the conversion planned to turn the barn into a workshop for a new cabinet making business he is about to start. You agreed to look at the place, to size it up for new wiring to power the sort of woodworking machinery that will be required, on a new metered supply. You went round a couple of days ago and costed it all up.

The materials would cost you approximately £650 and would include heavy duty switch boxes, fused circuits, cable conduits and supply box and meter. You reckon it would take you about 4 working days to do the job and you would expect to do it at the weekend. Your employer tends to expect you to work a lot of weekend days so you could not guarantee how many weekends it would actually take to finish. At worst, you should be able to complete the job in 6 weeks.

What you really need, however, and what prompted you to offer to do the job, is garage space. You have recently acquired a 1929 vintage racing car which needs secure, dry garaging where you can work on it. It does need some care and attention, and you are paying too much to garage it at the moment. You have no garage and you could not leave this wonderful old car out on the street.

It strikes you that you might be able to do a deal on garage space in return for giving your labour free. For that job you would expect an ordinary contracting electrician to charge about £250 in labour charges. You would have to charge your neighbour for the materials but you would be prepared to waive the normal trade mark up on materials of 20 per cent (in this case £130).

The rental you are paying at present for garaging space is £35 per month. What you would really like is free garaging for your old car, free access to the rear of your property through next door and free access to the garage and use of a small amount of light and power while working on your car. If pushed you could offer to help with any electrical repairs that might come up in the future.

THE GRAVEL PITS
Role Play 8

Time guide Up to 2½ hours, including 40 minutes for preparation and 40 minutes for review.

Participants 4 plus observers.

Equipment Desk, chairs and tables. (Trainers may wish to provide a choice of formal or informal seating for participants to choose their own preferred setting.) The complexity of this scenario means that extra meeting space may be required to accommodate more than one meeting simultaneously.

A copy of the general brief for all and a copy of the individual brief for each participant, and enough copies of all of them for the observers.

Notes for role players (Handout 4, page 48) if required. Observers' checklists (for an example see Handout 3, page 47).

Flipchart or whiteboard to record points from the debrief.

Video camera, tripod, recorder and TV monitor (if required).

LEARNING POINTS AND SKILLS PRACTISED

- All the general negotiation skills which include questioning, listening, proposing, bargaining and observation of non-verbal signals.
- Identification of common and conflicting interests and objectives.
- Suggesting creative options.
- Gaining agreement and commitment to mutually advantageous solutions.

Procedure See note on the procedure for conducting a role play (Checklist, page 49). Brief participants and allow 40 minutes for preparation. After the preparation time, participants may wish to conduct separate negotiations between each other before the meeting of all the interested parties. Brief observers and prepare the room to represent a hotel conference room. Allow play to continue for up to an hour and 10 minutes before allowing players to come out of role and begin the review.

Review See notes on feedback and review in Chapter 2 (Handouts 1 & 2, pages 45 and 46).

In particular, the group should try to answer the following questions as part of the review.

- How well were the participants prepared? Were their objectives clear?
- Was the final outcome satisfactory to all sides?
- Were all the factors considered? Did all the possible options emerge?
- How well did the various sides propose and bargain?
- Did each side achieve greatest benefit at least cost to the other?
- How effective were the various strategies that were adopted?

HANDOUT
Negotiation – the gravel pits

General brief for all

For many years there has been a gravel extraction operation going on in the wide river valley a few miles from the town. For the last few years this operation has been the business of one firm, River Gravel Ltd. The construction industry has suffered a downturn and demand has dropped as competition has increased. River Gravel have reduced their operation considerably over the last 18 months, so that they are now only dredging 2 small areas of their land at the point farthest away from the town.

The old workings are filled with water and heavily overgrown. There is, in total, about 100 hectares of flooded gravel pits and scrub. There are some 15 flooded pits in this area. River Gravel have now let it be known that they are interested in disposing of the land to realize some of its value. Their wish is to sell about half the land, some 7 pits and the surrounding banks, tracks and scrub, while retaining the capacity to develop the remaining area themselves at a later date for further extraction.

Over the years there have been several proposals from the local council and from people interested in developing the area for leisure use, none of which has come to anything. The land has little development value except as a leisure facility, and the cost of that would be high. A local company, Green Leisure Ltd, wish to take over some of the land and develop it for sailing, water-skiing and fishing. They have only limited means of financing both the purchase of the land and the development of the necessary facilities for a modern leisure attraction.

The local nature conservation group has an interest in the area. As the locality has reverted to scrub and freshwater lakes so an unusual habitat has developed for a whole range of wildlife including birds, butterflies and plants. In fact the area has a colony of an endangered snail and the particular old pit concerned may become a government-protected site (SSSI).

The local authority is interested in seeing that this land is put to some use and would like to see the development of more leisure facilities in the area, both to encourage visitors and to help employment in the area. It also has an interest in landfill sites for waste disposal.

In short, the gravel company wishes to reduce its overheads in maintaining fences and danger signs and realize some of the value of the unused land. The nature conservation group wishes to establish a reserve on as large an area as possible of these lakes. The local authority wishes to see the area developed and is looking for a waste disposal site.

A meeting has been called by the leisure company to explore ways of proceeding to everyone's advantage. It will take place in a local hotel. As one of the interested parties your task is to decide how to approach this problem, prepare for the meeting and decide if you should speak separately to any of the interested parties beforehand.

HANDOUT
Negotiation – the gravel pits

Brief for the chairman of River Gravel Ltd

You have been the principal shareholder and chairman of River
Gravel for 20 years. Times have never been so hard. You are now
forced to invest in new equipment to reduce the costs of extraction
or go out of business. Your only major asset is the land from which,
over the years, you have extracted your gravel. You know from
experience that the value of such land is low, even if a buyer can be
found. The main reason for this would appear to be that the cost of
development to a reasonable level is high and the returns from the
sort of development for which the land is suitable are small in the
early years. However, there was a case recently of the sale of some
old gravel workings in which the price given was £5000 per hectare.
If you could get that for your land you would have few problems left.
Your immediate needs now are for £100,000. You are already
borrowing more money from the bank than you would wish.

You are happy to examine any scheme that will raise the money you
require. You wish to dispose of approximately half of the now
derelict land, 48 hectares with 7 flooded pits. The other 53 hectares
you wish to retain, for, with the improved equipment that you wish
to buy, these pits could be put back into production. You will
consider any combination of purchase, rent or care and maintenance and associated options to buy, or payment by instalments.
The minimum you must achieve is £100,000 cash as soon as
possible; anything else, at this stage, would be a bonus. You do not
wish to throw away this asset and it is for that reason that you will
examine almost any scheme that people put forward. It would be
nice to have some share in any future leisure park and that might
form a part of a deal.

Your current costs for the care and maintenance of the area are approximately £5000 per year; a small amount but one you could do without.

The gravel you produce is currently costing you £5 per tonne to extract, wash and grade. Buyers will normally only pay for gravel delivered to where it is required and the margins are low. The normal price for your products is in the order of £8 a tonne. You would like to reduce the extraction costs – hence the need for new equipment. Transport costs at present account for a further £2.50 per tonne (on average) leaving you a margin of 50 pence a tonne which is really too small. If your customers were nearer, a better margin could be obtained. If you can acquire your new equipment, you calculate that your output capacity will be in the order of 200,000 tonnes per year. You estimate that you would reduce your extraction costs by up to £1 per tonne with the planned investment.

You need to get on with it and make a deal. You know the council has an interest in one part of the site for refuse disposal but its negotiations could take months.

You are looking forward to this meeting . . . there may be a chance to do some deals here.

HANDOUT
Negotiation – the gravel pits

Brief for the local authority official

You have been deputed to represent the local authority at the meeting called to discuss the future of the area of derelict gravel pits nearby. You are to protect the authority's interests and promote ideas that will forward their plans and requirements for the locality.

The authority is, in principle, keen to see the area improved. Planning permission for change of use to a leisure facility would rest on the satisfaction of various conditions concerning traffic, access, facilities and appearance but would not be difficult to achieve. The authority would be anxious to see that no one was prevented from developing the area because of planning difficulties.

There are small development grants available to help seed private ventures that are viewed by your authority as being of benefit to the local population. There is a possibility of there being a maximum of £20,000 available. In practice, unless the scheme will be of great significance in employment terms, half that figure would be a more realistic estimate of what might be available.

Your authority is also always looking for landfill sites for the disposal of refuse. It might be possible for one of the pits, on a plot of land of some $5\frac{1}{2}$ hectares, to be purchased for this purpose; it is separated from the rest by a road and a stretch of woodland. The authority would not wish to pay more than £2500 per hectare for this site. Your surveyors tell you that, geologically, the site presents no problems but that initial drainage might be difficult and the prevention of pollution downstream thereafter would be costly. This dictates the low price that the authority would be prepared to pay.

The authority actually buys large quantities of gravel for its roads and currently this is acquired from another part of the country. The amount spent on gravel and other aggregates last year was nearly 2 million pounds. About one third of that was for the type of gravel that is extracted locally. The price at present is £7.50 per tonne delivered. It would be good to encourage a local supplier if a suitable price or deal could be struck. About 90,000 tonnes are estimated to be this year's requirement.

HANDOUT
Negotiation – the gravel pits

Brief for the nature conservationist

You have had your eyes on the old gravel workings for some time. You are particularly keen to maintain and preserve the habitat of a species of freshwater snail that has established itself in these old gravel pits. In fact this is the largest and only significant colony of *Perforatella rubiginosa* in Northern Europe.

Apart from the snail the pits provide an excellent habitat for overwintering waterfowl; some 30 species have been observed here over the last few years. Several wild orchids have established themselves, there is a fledgling heronry and the scrub now provides an excellent environment for many species of birds, insects and small mammals. There has been an unconfirmed sighting of a red squirrel. You wish to arrange for a minimum of 4 of the old pits and about 15 hectares of land to be turned into a nature reserve. All this land is in the plot that River Gravel have indicated that they wish to dispose of.

You have a dedicated band of experienced volunteers who would be prepared to tidy the area, remove scrap and debris, plant more trees and encourage the development of specific habitats for specific species. They would also be able to build basic facilities for visitors (hides, walks, toilets, car parking and picnic areas). However, before any of that source of labour and goodwill could be used you need permanent access to the land and a reasonable prospect of the land being left alone.

You have available, for the establishment of nature reserves, some £10,000 and an annual income of about £2500. If you were able to proceed to create a reserve on the 15 hectares you have identified as being of most value, you estimate that you could raise some £20,000 by public subscription in the first year. You might not raise much money by a 'Save the Snail' campaign but wildfowl, small mammals and 'habitats' are much more appealing. Your discussions with the government lead you to believe that the area colonized by the snail could be designated a Site of Special Scientific Interest, an SSSI (3 hectares in area), and a grant of £4000 would be forthcoming if it were agreed.

Of the whole area that is up for sale, you are most concerned with the 3-hectare pit and surrounds in which *Perforatella* lives. The SSSI classification would be wonderful (and seems only a matter of time). A further 12 hectares form the core of the valuable habitat of which some 6 hectares are very vulnerable to any form of interference by man. The remaining 6 hectares could, conceivably, co-exist as a reserve with some limited exploitation for leisure. If you could achieve agreement on certain standards that should be maintained over the remainder of the site (or at least gain a right to be consulted about plans for the area) you would be delighted. In these circumstances you would be prepared to assist, with cash and labour, anyone trying to develop the site.

It is very pleasing to you that everyone with an interest in the site is to get together over it. There is a chance that you will make some progress towards your goals.

HANDOUT
Negotiation – the gravel pits

Brief for the director of Green Leisure Ltd

Your name is Green and you are the managing director of Green Leisure Ltd. Your company is a local one and you own a small sports complex in the town and a golf range nearby. For some time you have had your eye on the gravel pits with a view to developing them for watersports and fishing.

Now that River Gravel have announced that they wish to dispose of some of their land you have some ideas that you would like to see put into action. You can afford a maximum of £100,000 for purchase and development. Ideally, you would like the opportunity to buy as much of the land as possible but with an estimated initial £3000 per hectare development cost (on top of the purchase price) you are unlikely to be able to acquire more than a small part. Your best information suggests that the price for the land ought to be in the region of £3500–£4500 per hectare.

Your immediate plans, therefore, allow for the development of about 14 hectares, including 4 pits, (this excludes the potential Site of Special Scientific Interest for the snails) with approaches, parking, toilets, cafe and waterside hard standing and slipways as well as fish stocks and some sailing, water skiing equipment, etc. Your plans show that you should break even in about 3 years and you would not like to commit yourself to any further capital expenditure on land or development until these plans proved to be working. It would be good if you could have an option on the remaining land and you would be prepared to enter into joint ventures, rentals or care and maintenance deals if they were not too expensive.

You have already gathered that your name gives you an image. At your golf range you have made a great play of landscaping and providing a 'green' ambience to the place. You would be keen to extend the green image to this new project and are pleased that the local nature conservation group is interested in the area too. You do not want them stopping you from developing but you are more than happy to listen to what they have to say about the area in which they are particularly interested. It must be possible to agree about who has which bits of the area and also about some degree of cooperation on all or part of the area. You would gain an extra marketing advantage from appearing to be green.

You have called this meeting, and arranged for everyone to attend at the local hotel, because you see it as the surest way of being able to reconcile the conflicting interests and ensure that the maximum amount of financial resources should be available for various development possibilities on the site.

Chapter 5:

Appraisal role plays

Appraisal is part of the process of managing the performance of staff. It is the formal part of that process; an occasion on which the manager and his/her subordinate sit down together at regular intervals to discuss the subordinate's progress against previously agreed objectives. The requirements, objectives and standards for the coming period and the needs, wishes and aspirations of the subordinate as well as those of the organization form part of the discussions.

The purpose of the process is to reach agreement on the facts and on the plan for improving future performance including targets, standards, training and other assistance. Appraisal may also address the subject of potential in the subordinate and, therefore, the development needs of that individual. It is in essence a motivational process. It should involve constructive feedback about what has gone well and what has not. The whole should be based upon objectively observed facts and not opinion.

Appraisal, therefore, is an intimate, one to one, exercise in communication. To be successful the process and, in particular, the appraisal interview require the manager to possess the appropriate skills. One of the most effective techniques is to encourage the subordinate to carry out a self appraisal. People are often harder on themselves than is strictly necessary and this allows the appraising manager to start on a positive note. Self appraisal also necessitates reflection which is an essential part of learning. The other necessary skills include:

- questioning skills;
- listening effectively (including summarizing and reflecting);
- establishing rapport;
- controlling conversations;
- an understanding of body language;
- giving and receiving feedback;
- objective setting;
- gaining agreement and commitment;
- structuring the meeting;
- observation, interpretation and judgement;
- identifying training/development needs;
- reconciling individual and organizational needs.

The development of these skills requires practice for which role playing provides a safe environment. The following scenarios will give opportunities for all the above skills to be observed and practised. Other more specific skills are occasionally required and these emerge in one or more of the role plays.

THE FALTERING SECTION

Role Play 9

Time guide Up to 2 hours, including 30 minutes for preparation and 30 minutes for debrief.

Participants 2 plus observers.

Equipment Desk, chairs and tables. (Trainers may wish to provide a choice of formal or informal seating for participants to choose their own preferred setting.)

Copies of the general brief for all participants. Copies of the individual briefs for players of the appraisee and his manager. Copies of all the briefs for the observers.

Notes for role players (Handout 4, page 48) if required. Observers' checklists (for an example see Handout 3, page 47).

Flipchart or whiteboard to record points during the debrief.

Video camera, tripod, recorder and TV monitor (if required).

LEARNING POINTS AND SKILLS PRACTISED

- All the general appraisal skills such as questioning, listening, the giving of both positive and negative feedback and the observation of non-verbal signals.
- Gaining agreement for necessary changes to take place.
- The exploration of attitudes and perceptions.
- Suggesting creative alternatives to make agreement easier.
- Dealing with emotion and the resentment of criticism.
- The firm definition and agreement of plans, targets and training needs.

Procedure See notes on the conduct of role plays (Checklist, page 49). Brief participants and allow 30 minutes for preparation. Meanwhile brief the observers and set the room up to represent the manager's office. Allow play to continue for up to an hour before giving participants a little time to come out of role and begin the review.

Review See notes on feedback and review in Chapter 2 (Handouts 1 & 2, pages 45 and 46).

In particular, the group should try to answer the following questions as part of the review.

- Did the manager achieve his aim?
- How well did the manager encourage self appraisal?
- Was the need for change accepted and the plan agreed?
- How well did the manager involve the appraisee in the plan for the coming appraisal period? Were his ideas used?
- Who did most of the talking? Did the manager listen well?

HANDOUT
Appraisal – the faltering section

General brief for all

Plantsman Garden Centre has been trading for the last 15 years. It has grown from a nursery run by the present owner's father to a very substantial business turning over some £8.5 million last year. There has been a steady expansion over the last 5 years and the business has made good profits. The company now employs 210 staff, of whom some 50 per cent work part-time or at weekends only. One part of the recent developments has been the introduction of some good staff-management procedures. The appraisal scheme is one such development and all full-time staff are now appraised once a year. The latest venture has been to set up a fresh produce section. This has now been running for 9 months, managed by a new recruit, George Williams. Other developments have included the introduction of modern Electronic Point of Sale equipment so that statistics on stock, sales, profitability per section, trading patterns and the size of customers' purchases etc are easily obtained and monitored. There is also a linked, computerized purchasing system which allows easy monitoring of section heads' buying performance.

This interview will take place in the manager's office.

HANDOUT
Appraisal – the faltering section

Appraisee's brief

Your name is George Williams and you have worked at Plantsman for the last year. You were recruited specifically to set up and run the new produce section. You came from a major supermarket chain where you were a management trainee, working on the fresh produce side. You are 26 years old and single.

When you started it was made clear that the produce venture had to make a profit in the first year. Nine months since the section opened it is apparent that you will be lucky to break even if things continue as they are. Your turnover needs to be at least £95k for the year to make a small contribution to the business. It looks as if you will fall just short of £80k, which covers costs but no more. You are unhappy with the way that the new produce shop has been publicized and you are certain that the problem stems from there being too few customers walking through the door. You have bought well, locally, from wholesalers and to a small extent direct from the markets. Quality has been good and, given the stockturn, you believe you have provided a good product range to attract trade. In particular over the last 2 months, on the run-up to Christmas, your selection of exotic fruit and vegetables has been very well received and the margin on these products is high.

As you approach your appraisal with your boss you want to take the opportunity to get more publicity and approval to spend more on high quality, more unusual products to supplement the standard range. If the public were more aware of your existence and came to try you out they would find a good range of quality produce and then your turnover, you believe, would soar. You also want to take time to develop more local growers as suppliers for the standard fruit and vegetables. These would, you hope, give better service and better quality for the price than the major wholesalers. You have 3 full-time staff and 3 part-time. All are young and have been with you from the start. You have difficulty with most of them. Their timekeeping is poor and standards of housekeeping and display are poor. You are afraid to spend time away from the section for fear of what they might do in your absence. You have to tell them absolutely everything that has to be done. You would think they would pick up some of it. You wonder whether you should suggest some form of disciplinary action against them unless their attitude and performance improves.

You are a little concerned that your boss may raise the issue of your timekeeping. True, you have been late a few times after a heavy night or two, but you do put in a lot of extra hours in the evenings. Surely, as a manager, you can determine your own time schedule to some degree?

HANDOUT
Appraisal – the faltering section

Manager's brief

You are George Williams' boss and you recruited him a year ago to set up and run the new Produce Section. He seemed to be the best of the applicants by a long way. You told him at that time that he had to make a small trading profit in the first year, and that advertising and capital costs would not be included in his calculations for this first year. You have spent a great deal of money on advertising the new produce store, both inside the existing centre and in newspapers and even a short advert on local radio. It is apparent that the section will only just break even. If you then add capital and publicity costs, the whole thing begins to look unviable. It is, admittedly, early days and there are another three months to go to the year end but . . .

You are very pleased with the way that George buys. The price and quality do seem to be right. He does seem to have some very good ideas about how to make the section attractive and interesting. You do, however, have deep reservations about the amount of waste that is generated. Is he buying too much stock that cannot be sold before it deteriorates? Can we do something by offering staff discounted produce at the end of the day or the week? In any event you have to convince George that there may have to be changes in the stock/range/purchasing patterns.

Another problem which may be at the root of the rather poor performance of the section is George's handling of his staff. You feel that they are badly motivated and that they feel they are treated like second-class citizens. Indeed, your brother-in-law, whose daughter, your niece, works in the section at weekends spoke to you a couple of weeks ago asking 'What's up with this guy George? Has he got a power complex or something? Jenny is thinking of leaving even though she can do with the money. He ought to be able to get on with a bunch of sixth formers.'

You are determined to get George to see that he has a problem when it comes to dealing with staff. Perhaps he needs some inter-personal skills training. Poorly led staff will not treat customers well. You are also concerned about the example he sets. His timekeeping is not good, and he has appeared a few times looking very much the worse for wear from the night before.

In short you think that his product knowledge and experience of the trade are excellent. These, however, need directing and more detailed planning of purchasing requirements needs to be done. His people skills are not good and must be improved, and you want to warn him about his timekeeping and late nights.

THE ZEALOUS EMPLOYEE

Role Play 10

Time guide Up to 1½ hours, including 25 minutes for preparation and 30 minutes for review.

Participants 2 plus observers.

Equipment Desk, chairs and tables. (Trainers may wish to provide a choice of formal or informal seating for participants to choose their own preferred setting.)

Copies of the general brief for all participants. Copies of the individual briefs for players of the appraisee and his manager. Copies of all the briefs for the observers.

Notes for role players (Handout 4, page 48) if required. Observers' checklists (for an example see Handout 3, page 47).

Flipchart or whiteboard to record points during the debrief.

Video camera, tripod, recorder and TV monitor (if required).

LEARNING POINTS AND SKILLS PRACTISED

- All the general appraisal skills such as questioning, listening, the giving of both positive and negative feedback and the observation of non-verbal signals.
- The need to probe attitudes and perceptions to help to establish underlying causes of behaviour.
- Suggesting creative alternatives to make agreement to plans, targets and standards for the future easier to reach.
- The need for sensitivity in a touchy situation, and dealing with strong characters, emotion and resentment of criticism.
- The firm definition and agreement of plans, targets and training needs.

Procedure See notes on the conduct of role plays (Checklist, page 49). Brief participants and allow up to 25 minutes for preparation. Meanwhile, brief observers and lay out the room to represent the administration manager's office. Allow play to continue for up to 30 minutes and then give a little time for participants to come out of role before starting the review.

Review See notes on feedback and review in Chapter 2 (Handouts 1 & 2, pages 45 and 46).

In particular, the group should try to answer the following questions as part of the review.

- Did the manager succeed in his aim?
- Was agreement reached over the need for change, and over the plan for the coming appraisal period?
- What reactions might be expected from the employee in this situation and how might they be handled?
- How well did the manager encourage honest self appraisal?

HANDOUT
Appraisal – the zealous employee

General brief for all

Mary Holden is a data entry operator at Coversure Insurance. Coversure is a large national insurance organization specializing in the motor, marine and household insurance markets. There are 250 staff at the head office, many of whom are part-time. Five of the 14 staff who work on the data entry VDUs are full-time, including the supervisor, Jenny. Jenny is 19 years old and only recently appointed to the supervisor's role.

The data entry section is part of the administration department and the administration manager is responsible for a total of 25 staff, including their appraisal. The data entry section is responsible for entering on to the computer system all the necessary information to run not only the company administration system but also all data to set up, obtain payment of premiums, and generally monitor the insurance policies of all their many customers. The system in use has been in operation for about 6 months. Before that, the previous system had been in use for about 8 years.

The work is repetitive and fairly undemanding except that it requires the ability to key in large quantities of data in both numeric and text form quickly and accurately. The system monitors the speed of entry of individual operators by key depressions and a regular weekly report appears as a means of monitoring performance. This system is not popular but it does provide some measure for management to control performance.

HANDOUT
Appraisal – the zealous employee

Appraisee's brief

You are Mary Holden, a data entry operator at Coversure Insurance. You have worked there for 8 years, ever since the old computer system was installed. You joined shortly after your husband died. You work full time and the companionship and interest that work provides mean a great deal for you. You are 56 and live alone and you have no close family so your job is to a very real extent your life.

You believe quite strongly that there are a lot of things that could be improved around here and it is very frustrating that you are not given the opportunity to put things right. For a start you would really like to have a go at some of the silly kids that are working here now: they appear to have no sense and no discipline.

You believe in doing a fair day's work and, having been brought up in the old school (a hard school), you have great respect for the bosses and the company. They provide your livelihood after all. You are good at your job and your key depressions and accuracy are among the best in the section, but you are finding it increasingly difficult to do a good job with this new computer system, and all the chatting and joking that is going on make it even more difficult. Only last week you told a group of the part-time youngsters to be quiet and do some work for a change. They took exception to this and a bit of a row ensued. Eventually the administration manager came and sorted it out. You feel quite strongly that you could do better than this young Jenny, the new 'so-called' supervisor. There have been several occasions when you have done her job for her by keeping the young girls in line. Like the last memorable occasion they have been rude several times and you have spoken to your manager about this and the inadequacies of your supervisor. This was some weeks ago now.

Since the new computer system came into use, you have really struggled to keep up your output and accuracy. You find the distraction of the other staff a real pain as you find that you are having to concentrate much harder than you ever had to. You have started to suffer from headaches although a recent eye test was reassuring. You are quite anxious about all this as your job depends on your ability to key quickly and accurately, so you don't want the company to know anything about it.

You see this appraisal as the ideal opportunity to put the case for more responsibility and to start to have things run the way they should be.

HANDOUT
Appraisal – the zealous employee

Manager's brief

Mary Holden has worked for Coversure for 8 years as a data entry operator. She is 56 years old. She is hard-working and extremely conscientious. Her timekeeping and attendance are excellent. Her work is quick and accurate and she always keeps her part of the office clean and tidy. You are, however, concerned over her ability to get on with other staff. Only last week you were called to deal with a problem when Mary had shouted across the office at a group of other staff to stop chatting and get on with their work. There is little doubt in your mind that she had taken upon herself a role that was not hers to adopt and that, in any case, there was no real need to react as the level of chat in the office is very rarely a barrier to reasonable output.

Mary did come to see you a little while ago to complain about the behaviour of the other staff and in passing she had a swipe at Jenny, the new young supervisor. Jenny was appointed because of her keenness, enthusiasm and real skills in instructing the high turnover of young part-time staff in the intricacies of the new hi-tech VDUs and the procedures to be followed. You have seen no reason to criticize her performance and she seems to deal very well with the majority of the staff who are near her own age. You can see that she might have difficulty with Mary, who is so much older than she is.

You are very pleased with the quality of Mary's work on a routine level, but she is causing a lot of aggravation by her assumption that she knows best and that she has the right to tell others what to do. You feel that her attitude is in no small way responsible for the high turnover that you are experiencing in the section.

You are determined to get to the bottom of the problem and to get Mary to agree to a change of behaviour towards her supervisor and her workmates.

THE EMPLOYEE NEAR RETIREMENT

Role Play 11

Time Guide Up to 1¼ hours, including 20 minutes for preparation and 20 minutes for review.

Participants 2 plus observers.

Equipment Desk, chairs and tables.(Trainers may wish to provide a choice of formal or informal seating for participants to choose their own preferred setting.)

Copies of the general brief for all participants. Copies of the individual briefs for players of the appraisee and his manager. Copies of all the briefs for the observers.

Notes for role players (Handout 4, page 48) if required. Observers' checklists (for an example see Handout 3, page 47).

Flipchart or whiteboard to record points during the debrief.

Video camera, tripod, recorder and TV monitor (if required).

LEARNING POINTS AND SKILLS PRACTISED

- All the general appraisal skills which include questioning, listening, the giving of both positive and negative feedback and the observation of non-verbal signals.
- The exploration of attitudes and perceptions.
- Suggesting creative alternatives to make agreement easier to reach.
- The remotivation of an employee near to retirement.
- The firm definition and agreement of plans, targets and training needs.

Procedure See notes on conducting a role play (Checklist, page 49). Brief the participants and allow time for preparation. Meanwhile brief observers and set the room up to represent the manager's office. Allow play to continue for up to 30 minutes before giving a little time for participants to come out of role and start the review.

Review See notes on feedback and review in Chapter 2 (Handouts 1 & 2, pages 45 and 46).

In particular, the group should try to answer the following questions as part of the review.

- Was the employee left with the right overall impression?
- Was there agreement about the need for change and about what was required in the future?
- How well was the employee's self appraisal encouraged?
- Did the manager listen and question effectively?
- Was the plan for the future likely to be effective for long?

HANDOUT
Appraisal – the employee near retirement

General brief for all

Turnall Engineering has been in business for 30 years providing a precision engineering service to a range of larger manufacturers in the region. They act principally as sub-contractors, producing parts for final assembly elsewhere. The quality of their work, the speedy service and their willingness to make very short production runs at competitive prices are seen as the basis for their continued success. Turnall now employs 160 people and included in this number is a drawing and design office staff of 6. With one exception, they are all experienced staff with long service. There is one trainee recruited this year who is learning the ropes and working with others on each project as it appears. Their work, providing drawings and instructions for the shop floor, has been critical in enabling the company to provide the service it does both in terms of delivery times and in terms of really economical manufacturing methods.

The drawing office staff are the only people in the company, other than the directors and the four senior managers, to be included in a profit-sharing bonus scheme. Their earnings are good, but they work hard for them.

There are plans afoot to replace some of the machinery in the workshop. In the next few months, plans must be produced for the introduction of this machinery. The plans must incorporate the specifications of the machinery, the new extension to accommodate it and the new layout, and there is a need to minimize the disruption to production during the changeover.

All this will mean changes in the drawing office and the staff there will have to get to know the capabilities and limitations of the new equipment very quickly.

Appraisal is an annual event and the manager has arranged a meeting, in a few minutes, with Harold Brown from the drawing office.

HANDOUT
Appraisal – the employee near retirement

Appraisee's brief

You are Harold Brown, aged 58. You work in the drawing and design office of Turnall Engineering where you have been for the last 27 years. You are the longest serving member of the drawing office team of 6. Your manager is the production manager who has been with the firm almost as long as you.

Over the last year your life has changed dramatically. Your last daughter (one of 6 children) has left home, your mortgage is finally paid off and your finances are quite secure. Your pension is also secure and you are contemplating retiring a little early in a few years' time. You are not sure when, and you would miss the friends you have made at work.

Work has become far less important to you, and you are wondering what to do with the rest of your life. There is no likelihood of any promotion, and your job has become routine. You want eventually to move to North Devon, where you want to indulge your passion for growing orchids (something you have been unable to do very well here through lack of space for a decent greenhouse).

You have been working the required hours, have done everything that has been asked of you but you do not see the point in working flat out any more. Life's too short and there are other things that interest you now. There have been two occasions lately where you have had a brush with your manager when you felt you were being pressed too much. On both occasions longer deadlines were accepted.

You are about to go for your appraisal interview and you are interested to see what will be said. It may influence your decision about retirement if your manager has a go at you.

© David Turner 1992, published by Kogan Page

HANDOUT
Appraisal – the employee near retirement

Manager's brief

You are Harold's manager, the production manager of Turnall, and have been for more years than you care to remember. He has always been a very conscientious worker and a valuable member of the drawing office team. He is the longest serving member of the team and is now 58 years old. His knowledge of the equipment and its capabilities is excellent and much valued.

This year you have a problem with his appraisal. His work has slipped over the year. He is not prepared to put in any extra effort even when big orders are at stake and twice recently he has refused to accept deadlines that you set him. You amended them at the time but you now want to know what is the matter with him. Admittedly, you cannot criticize the quality of the work that he does, it is just as good as it always was, but there just isn't the interest or enthusiasm there any more. He does enough to get by but no more. Some others in the office are beginning to mutter that he is not pulling his weight and his attitude is beginning to disrupt the office and affect others. His timekeeping and absence record are above reproach but you wish you could retrieve the commitment to the work that he used to have. You wonder whether there is anything in the new investment plans that would 'hook' his old enthusiasm.

COMPETENCE WITHOUT CONFIDENCE

Role Play 12

Time Guide Up to 1½ hours, including preparation and review.

Participants 2 plus observers.

Equipment Desk, chairs and tables. (Trainers may wish to provide a choice of formal or informal seating for participants to choose their own preferred setting.)

Copies of the appropriate briefs for each participant and copies of both for the observers.

Notes for role players (Handout 4, page 48) if required. Observers' checklists (for an example see Handout 3, page 47).

Flipchart or whiteboard to record points during the debrief.

Video camera, tripod, recorder and TV monitor (if required).

LEARNING POINTS AND SKILLS PRACTISED

- All the general appraisal skills such as questioning, listening, the giving of both positive and negative feedback and the observation of non-verbal signals.
- Gaining agreement for necessary changes to take place.
- The need to make the employee accept the value of the contribution they make by the use of self appraisal.
- The exploration of attitudes and perceptions.
- The firm definition and agreement of plans, targets and training needs.

Procedure See notes on the conduct of a role play (Checklist, page 49). Brief the participants and allow time for preparation. Meanwhile, brief the observers and arrange furniture to represent the manager's office. Allow play to continue for up to 30 minutes before giving a little time for players to come out of role before starting the review.

Review See notes on feedback and review in Chapter 2 (Handouts 1 & 2, pages 45 and 46).

In particular, the group should try to answer the following questions as part of the review.

- Was the employee left with the right overall impression?
- How effective was the self appraisal?
- Was a plan for future performance and development agreed?
- How well did the manager listen and question?
- Did both people achieve what they wanted?

HANDOUT
Appraisal – competence without confidence

Brief for the manager

You are the manager of a branch of a national retail operation. You have 6 supervisors responsible for different sections of the business reporting to you. Chris Howard is one of these supervisors, aged 34, and recently promoted to run the giftware section. This promotion occurred just before the Christmas season when the previous job-holder was sacked for pilfering.

It was a very difficult situation but Chris has coped with it extremely well, picking up the layouts and plans very quickly and recognizing the problems and priorities as they arose. You are very impressed with the way the section and its staff were handled and you have every confidence that Chris will make a very good supervisor.

The 3 full-time and 2 part-time staff seem to like and get on with their new supervisor and there has been no hint of a problem there. But Chris has begun to look a bit tired and has had a few days off sick in the last couple of weeks.

Since Christmas, trade in the giftware section has been very slack, as expected, and now is the time to lay the plans for the spring and summer seasons. You are a bit disappointed that, so far, there have been no ideas or suggestions forthcoming from Chris. You did see a lot of creative ideas in the pre-Christmas displays and you want to explore how Chris would like to see the section develop over the next few months.

Timekeeping, product knowledge, appearance, etc, are perfectly good but you are concerned about Chris's ability to self-start, to take the initiative or to 'go for it'. It strikes you that there might be a lack of confidence here – quite unjustifiably in your opinion.

In short, Chris seems to have a great deal of potential, did a great job over Christmas, and seems to do all the right things. If only there was a bit more coming forward, a willingness to voice an opinion or put forward ideas.

It is the time of year for appraisals and you must address these issues at Chris's appraisal interview in a few minutes.

HANDOUT
Appraisal – competence without confidence

Brief for the employee

You are Chris Howard, aged 34, and you have been working in this branch of the retail organization for the last 4 years, full-time. You were promoted to be the supervisor of the giftware section just a few weeks before Christmas. You have 3 full-time and 2 part-time staff working for you.

You thoroughly enjoy the job but you do feel very unsure of yourself when you are dealing with salesmen or your manager, and you find getting your staff to do things very stressful. You have a good knowledge of the product range and you like to see things looking nice. Your manager has always been very pleased with the displays and the way that you and your staff handle customers. The Christmas period was hectic and you are not sure how you coped with it at all but your people were a great help and you got by somehow. The level of trade since then has been very low.

There are a whole series of different product lines in ceramics, fabrics and wood that you would like to see on the section but you feel that now is probably the wrong time to start asking and you are not sure how your manager would accept suggestions from you anyway. In fact you are not really sure where your responsibility ends and your manager's begins. Being new as a supervisor you are reluctant to push your ideas.

Your main idea comes from comments from several customers who would appear to be interested in tapestry and needlework supplies. The nearest decent source of supply for these people is some 20 miles away and they would like something nearer. You are hesitating about whether to mention this to anyone.

You are dreading this appraisal interview. You think you could do things better but you don't know how. At the moment you are just pleased that nothing seems to have gone drastically wrong. The last few days you have had sleepless nights worrying about it and how your manager is going to rate you. Your family is dependent on your salary and things are very tight, so the promotion helped. You need to keep going in the supervisor's job even though it causes you a lot of worry . . . and you want to prove you can do it. Perhaps you will be able to ask the manager to be clearer about what you are expected to do.

THE UNCOMMITTED WAREHOUSEMAN

Role Play 13

Time Guide Up to 1½ hours, including preparation and review.

Participants 2 plus observers.

Equipment Desk, chairs and tables. (Trainers may wish to provide a choice of formal or informal seating for participants to choose their own preferred setting.)

Copies of the appropriate briefs for each participant and copies of both for the observers.

Notes for role players (Handout 4, page 48) if required. Observers' checklists (for an example see Handout 3, page 47).

Flipchart or whiteboard to record points during the debrief.

Video camera, tripod, recorder and TV monitor (if required).

LEARNING POINTS AND SKILLS PRACTISED

- All the general appraisal skills including questioning, listening, the giving of both positive and negative feedback and the observation of non-verbal signals.
- The need to explore reasons for the observed behaviour.
- Gaining agreement for necessary changes to take place.
- The exploration of attitudes and perceptions and identifying what will motivate the appraisee to change.
- The firm definition and agreement of standards, targets and training needs.

Procedure See notes on the conduct of a role play (Checklist, page 49). Brief the participants and allow time for preparation. Meanwhile, brief the observers and arrange furniture to represent the manager's office. Allow play to continue for up to 30 minutes before giving a little time for players to come out of role before starting the review.

Review See notes on feedback and review in Chapter 2 (Handouts 1 & 2, pages 45 and 46).

In particular, the group should try to answer the following questions as part of the review.

- How successful was the manager in putting his message across?
- Was the employee left with the right overall impression?
- Were the standards and target for the coming period clearly set out, understood and agreed?
- Who did most of the talking? Did the employee get the chance to put across what he was looking for?
- How well did the manager listen and question?

HANDOUT
Appraisal – the uncommitted warehouseman

Brief for the manager

John Holdfast is 22 and has worked in the Cash and Carry for the last 4 years. You are the warehouse manager and have been his manager for the last 18 months. For various reasons you have never actually sat down to talk to him, except when you first joined, so this appraisal will be the first opportunity for you to talk to him in any depth about his work.

Generally you are disappointed in him. He seems lazy, likes to wander off and chat, and his sickness record is not good. He has had 12 days off sick this year, 8 of them single odd days and always Mondays. His work is adequate, just, but a bit slapdash. Several errors in documentation (shortages in deliveries not reported, damaged goods returned not properly consigned etc) are thought to have been due to him, but you can't prove it.

He does spend quite a bit of time wandering around the Cash and Carry and is often found helping other people. Other managers have complained about his wasting their staff's time and of his attitude to customers. He seems to avoid customers and dodges having to deal with them, pushing them off on to somebody else if he can. He really should be able to deal with them properly since his work takes him back and forth from the warehouse to the sales floor.

He is a likeable chap and seems to get on well with most people and, given a simple manual job to do, will get stuck in and get it done. His timekeeping is good although his attendance/sickness is not so good. His work standards and accuracy are pretty poor and somehow he seems to lack commitment. He spends much too much time away from his work.

You have arranged to see him for his appraisal in your office in a few minutes.

HANDOUT
Appraisal – the uncommitted warehouseman

Brief for the employee

Your name is John Holdfast, you are 22, and have worked in the warehouse of the Cash and Carry for the last 4 years.

Your timekeeping is good, and you have really only had a few days sick. Some of those days have been Mondays after you have celebrated your win at football in the Sunday afternoon league.

You work well enough for the warehouse, but you don't believe in putting in long hours or overdoing things. There are, after all, other things in life apart from work and the wages aren't that good, are they?

Your new wife (you were married 3 months ago) would like you to get a better job since the baby is due in a couple of months' time. There doesn't seem to be much chance of promotion where you are, and anyway you are not looking for responsibility.

You always get on well with the rest of the staff and enjoy a laugh and a chat. You do not like dealing with customers and try to avoid them if you can. When questioned you tend to try to fob them off with someone else; you are employed as a warehouseman, not as a sales assistant.

You are a bit bored with the routine in the warehouse. There is always something new arriving and keeping track of all the products is difficult. Still, the others seem to know what's what, so you can get by by asking them. You would rather spend your time getting 'stuck in' to some decent task like loading or unloading vehicles or, as you have started to do, learning a bit more about what others do around the Cash and Carry.

Now that you are about to be appraised by your manager, whom you have never had a lot of time for (you are for ever being chased), what you really want to achieve is a decent bonus this year to keep the wife happy, and the chance to do something different or more interesting. The interview is due to take place shortly in the manager's office.

THE BRILLIANT TECHNICIAN
Role Play 14

Time Guide Up to 1½ hours, including time for preparation and review.

Participants 2 plus observers.

Equipment Desk, chairs and tables. (Trainers may wish to provide a choice of formal or informal seating for participants to choose their own preferred setting.)

Copies of the appropriate briefs for each participant and copies of both for the observers.

Notes for Role Players (Handout 4, page 48) if required.
Observers' checklists (for an example see Handout 3, page 47).

Flipchart or whiteboard to record points during the debrief.

Video camera, tripod, recorder and TV monitor (if required).

LEARNING POINTS AND SKILLS PRACTISED

- All the general appraisal skills such as questioning, listening, the giving of both positive and negative feedback and the observation of non-verbal signals.
- Gaining acceptance for the need to change and agreement for the necessary changes to take place.
- The exploration of attitudes and perceptions and identifying what will motivate the appraisee to change.
- The need to explore reasons for the observed behaviour.
- The firm definition and agreement of required standards and training needs.

Procedure See notes on conducting a role play (Checklist, page 49). Brief the participants and allow time for preparation. Meanwhile brief the observers and arrange the room to represent the manager's office. Allow play to continue for up to 30 minutes before giving a few moments for participants to come out of role before beginning the review.

Review See notes on feedback and review in Chapter 2 (Handouts 1 & 2, pages 45 and 46).

In particular, the group should try to answer the following questions as part of the review.

- Was the employee left with the right overall impression?
- Did the manager extract a worthwhile self appraisal?
- Did the appraisee recognise the areas in which improvement is necessary?
- Was the need for change accepted? If not, why not?
- Was a plan for the coming appraisal period made and agreed?
- How well did the manager question and listen?

HANDOUT
Appraisal – the brilliant technician

Brief for the manager

You are the manager of a division in a large national company. Your division is responsible to the main company for the specification, writing, production and commissioning of software for use in production control and automation systems.

You have a team of 12 staff engaged on anything up to 10 separate projects simultaneously. You operate in small project teams using people with the necessary skills for each separate project. Most of your staff are involved in 3 or 4 projects at once.

One person, Michelle, is involved in them all. She is, quite literally, invaluable to you and the rest of the team, as her ability to recognize and diagnose problems in software programs is amazing. The mistakes and inconsistencies seem to jump out at her and she is able to construct ways of making programs 'sit up and beg' in remarkably short periods of time. She is used as a trouble shooter and any project with gremlins, glitches or bugs in the system is passed to Michelle for her to sort out.

Unfortunately, her manner towards the rest of the team is very condescending and off-hand. She manages to put the back up of everyone who comes to her with a problem. She appears contemptuous of anyone not able to follow her reasoning, which she insists on spelling out at great length on every possible occasion. Her ability to communicate effectively is poor. Not only can she not seem to relate to others but she also seems incapable of explaining anything in any but the most complex way. The result is that people are reluctant to go and see her with a problem until they have spent many hours trying to resolve it themselves in an attempt to avoid using her skills altogether. This, of course, delays projects.

You have to keep her with you, since many problems would be either insoluble or extremely costly to solve without her. You would like to use her to pass on some of her diagnostic skills to others in the team but there is no way that she would succeed in doing so with her current attitude and lack of communication skills.

Michelle is able to get through huge amounts of work and never seems happier than when engrossed in a really complex problem. Her results, accuracy and success in producing first-time solutions are first class.

You are due to see her for her appraisal in your office shortly.

HANDOUT
Appraisal – the brilliant technician

Brief for the employee

You are Michelle Spencer and you work for a division of a large company whose task it is to specify, write, produce and commission software for use in production control and automation systems.

The rest of the 12-strong team operate in small project groups, formed of people with the relevant skills for the project. You tend to operate alone as the overseer of the software programing. Any problems arising during the commissioning phase, or difficulties in writing programs to achieve particular results, are brought to you to resolve. You have demonstrated time and again your ability to recognize or diagnose errors and problems very quickly. In addition, you have always been able to see ways round problems that others have found great difficulty with.

The rest of the team may be good at selling, good production engineers or analysts but they are certainly not good programers. You keep trying to tell them where they are going wrong but they seem to resent it. You used to get involved in all the projects at an early stage to advise on programing but this is happening less now and you seem to get only the really difficult problems that the others have tried to solve and failed. You now seem to spend your time digging them out of the mire.

You are very proud of what you have done and of the time and money you have saved the company with your problem-solving skills. You really enjoy the challenge of a difficult problem to solve and have excellent powers of concentration that help you to arrive at better solutions quicker than everyone else. You could reduce the errors in programing and speed successful commissioning if people would consult you earlier, but they seem to resent your abilities.

As you approach your appraisal with your manager you have decided that you would like to tackle this problem and try to get involved more in the early stages so that you can keep a closer eye on the programing. This way, when programs and systems are being commissioned, you will not have to spend so much time, under pressure, trying to get them to work properly. Prevention is, after all, better than cure and this should reduce project length. You want your manager to recognize the contribution you make and to formalize the special position that your skills entitle you to.

THE FRIENDLY SERVICE ENGINEER

Role Play 15

Time Guide Up to 1½ hours, including time for preparation and review.

Participants 2 plus observers.

Equipment Desk, chairs and tables. (Trainers may wish to provide a choice of formal or informal seating for participants to choose their own preferred setting.)

Copies of the appropriate briefs for each participant and copies of both for the observers.

Notes for role players (Handout 4, page 48) if required. Observers' checklists (for an example see Handout 3, page 47).

Flipchart or whiteboard to record points during the debrief.

Video camera, tripod, recorder and TV monitor (if required).

LEARNING POINTS AND SKILLS PRACTISED

- All the general appraisal skills including questioning, listening, the giving of both positive and negative feedback and the observation of non-verbal signals.
- Recognition of the impact of current behaviour and gaining acceptance for the need to change and agreement for the necessary changes to take place.
- The exploration of attitudes and perceptions and identifying what will motivate the appraisee to change.
- The need to explore reasons for the observed behaviour.
- The firm definition and agreement of standards and training needs.

Procedure See notes on conducting a role play (Checklist, page 49). Brief the participants and allow about 30 minutes for preparation. Meanwhile brief the observers and set up the furniture to represent the manager's office. Allow play to continue for up to 30 minutes and then give a little time for participants to come out of role before commencing the review.

Review See notes on feedback and review in Chapter 2 (Handouts 1 & 2, pages 45 and 46).

In particular, the group should try to answer the following questions as part of the review.

- Did the manager succeed in putting across his message?
- Were the required standards for the future clearly stated? Was a clear plan agreed for monitoring future performance?
- Was the need for improvement accepted?
- Was there agreement about the required actions?
- How well did the manager question and listen?

HANDOUT
Appraisal – the friendly service engineer

Brief for the manager

You are the regional service manager for Packroll, a company producing packaging machinery and materials-handling equipment. The company maintains a nationwide servicing and maintenance team which repairs and maintains the company's products under warranty or under contract for older machinery. This service team is seen as being an important contact with customers as a means of encouraging future sales.

One of your service engineers, Steve Walsh, is causing you some problems. He is a very cheerful individual and is soon on first name terms with everyone he meets. He has a very friendly disposition and enjoys a chat and a gossip with his customers. This has given rise to one or two complaints about charges for the time spent on site.

His appearance is scruffy, his overalls could stand up on their own and the van he drives is always a tip. He joined the company 5 years ago but his engineering knowledge has advanced no further in that time. There are still jobs that he has to pass on to other engineers. His general performance is disappointing. His paperwork is always scruffy, sometimes inadequate and often late. This gives the accounts section real headaches.

He is rarely sick, can be relied upon to keep to the schedule of service visits and responds well to calls for emergency repairs. The quality of the work he does, however, is slapdash and there have been several cases of complaints about faults that have been missed on inspections. All these have been dismissed by him with comments such as 'Ah well, you can't win 'em all'.

You have had a go at him several times over the last 2 years and each time his performance has improved for a while but it soon slips back to its original level.

You are concerned that his slapdash approach is damaging the company's reputation with some of the customers he visits. In fact, you know of one case where one of Steve's customers purchased a large piece of equipment from a competitor. Hitherto they had a factory full of your machinery.

You are about to conduct his appraisal.

HANDOUT
Appraisal – the friendly service engineer

Brief for the employee

You are Steve Walsh, aged 47, and you are a service engineer for Packroll, a company producing packaging machinery and materials handling equipment. You spend your time working to a schedule of service visits for customers on your patch who have machinery under maintenance contract or warranty. There are occasional emergency repairs to be attended to, which give the opportunity for a bit of overtime. (You prefer not to do much of that, though, because you are the barman at the local Working Men's Club for three or four nights a week.)

You joined the company 5 years ago, and you have a fully equipped van which the company provides with which you cover a large patch spreading over 5 counties. You work from home, arranging your visits direct with customers by phone and reporting weekly, again by phone, to your regional manager.

Your manager visits you about once every 6 weeks and is a bit of a stickler. You have been told off a few times about your appearance, the state of your van and the amount of gossiping you are supposed to do. As far as you are concerned, your appearance is fine. You are an engineer and you don't need to go to work in a suit, collar and tie. You are bound to get a bit dirty, after all. Your van is where you work all day. It is your rest area as well as a means of transport. You tidy it up and give it a wash now and then but you are pretty busy. You cannot agree with your manager about the chatting; you keep having your ear banged about the need to keep the company in the eye of the customer to encourage future sales, so you go out of your way to create a friendly relationship with as many of the customers' staff as you can.

There have been a couple of complaints recently about some faults that you missed. But there have got to be a few mistakes, haven't there; we're all human.

You enjoy the job. It gets you out and about to meet people and you like to think that you have some good friends among your customers. But it is only a job. It pays quite well, so you make an effort to keep to the service schedules. You don't want any promotion, you are quite happy to plod on with this for a few more years. You can get by quite well so you don't want the effort of going for more training or qualifications.

You are about to see the regional manager for your appraisal.

HOPING FOR PROMOTION

Role Play 16

Time Guide Up to 1½ hours, including time for preparation and review.

Participants 2 plus observers.

Equipment Desk, chairs and tables. (Trainers may wish to provide a choice of formal or informal seating for participants to choose their own preferred setting.)

Copies of the appropriate briefs for each participant and copies of both for the observers.

Notes for role players (Handout 4, page 48) if required. Observers' checklists (for an example see Handout 3, page 47).

Flipchart or whiteboard to record points during the debrief.

Video camera, tripod, recorder and TV monitor (if required).

LEARNING POINTS AND SKILLS PRACTISED

- All the general appraisal skills which include questioning, listening, the giving of both positive and negative feedback and the observation of non-verbal signals.
- The exploration of the employee's needs and aspirations.
- The agreement of a plan to involve the employee more in order to motivate them to continue to perform well.
- The use of self appraisal to help gain acceptance by the individual of their limitations.

Procedure See notes on conducting role plays (Checklist, page 49). Brief the participants and allow time for preparation. Meanwhile brief the observers and set up the room to represent the manager's office. Allow play to continue for up to 30 minutes and then give a few moments for the participants to come out of role before starting the review.

Review See notes on conducting a role play in Chapter 2 (Handouts 1 & 2, pages 45 and 46).

In particular, the group should try to answer the following questions as part of the review.

- How well did the manager get the employee to accept their limitations? Did he encourage self appraisal?
- How well did the manager question and listen during the interview?
- Was the employee left with the correct overall impression?
- Was there an agreed plan for the future that aimed at retaining the employee's motivation and self esteem?

HANDOUT
Appraisal – hoping for promotion

Brief for the manager

You are the sales manager for the company and your sales office manager is Pat Harrison. The sales office employs a staff of 8 working on telephones, following leads and processing orders from the salesmen in the field.

The office runs very efficiently. Mistakes are very rare, messages are punctiliously passed on and orders are almost invariably correctly transcribed and correct detail seems to be a matter of pride with them. This must all be due to Pat who is an absolute stickler for detail, checking and accuracy.

You know that Pat is keen for promotion. Unfortunately, you believe that the ceiling has been reached and that there is no scope for further promotion. As an administrator with a few experienced staff Pat has few equals but in different circumstances, with a requirement to plan, to anticipate and to manage a wider range of staff you feel there would be great difficulties. The style of approach to staff is very old-fashioned and staff turnover has been a real problem. The ability to see beyond the system and the rules is very limited and imagination, flexibility or compromise are concepts that have little meaning to Pat.

In your appraisal interview you want to ensure that the current high performance is maintained and you also want to get Pat to accept that there really isn't anywhere else to go and that there will be no promotion. This may be quite difficult because the consistently good personal reports and the reputation that the office has will have raised expectations.

There are a few things that you can think of to give Pat more interest and maybe a sense of value once the issue of promotion prospects is out of the way. For instance, there is a new computerized order processing system in the offing and it will need careful handling, with new procedures to be written. Pat ought to be able to handle this and it might keep interest and enthusiasm alive. In addition there are several sets of statistical sales records that you keep that you could delegate (call rates, costs per order, product performance, etc).

Your biggest problem will be getting Pat to accept that there will be no promotion. You need to emphasize the value placed on the current efficiency of the office and give a reason for that performance to continue.

HANDOUT
Appraisal – hoping for promotion

Brief for the employee

You are Pat Harrison, manager of the sales office, and you have been doing the job for some considerable time. You have 8 staff involved in processing orders received from the field sales force, following up and passing out leads generated centrally and keeping the administration afloat.

You are very pleased with the way things are going. Your staff have, at last, come round to your ways. Everything runs very smoothly thanks to the system of checks, double checks and inspection that you have instigated. It was a problem to start with, but now you have managed to find some staff who can do the job your way, the office works well. You jump on any mistakes very quickly and you insist on very strict discipline in the office.

When you started there were a group of people who you thought were an intelligent bunch. But they did not seem to be able to grasp the need for tight control and constant attention to detail and checks. They have all now gone and your current staff is much more reliable and has the right degree of respect for you and the systems you have imposed. They do seem to be clock watchers, however, and they don't seem to have any great loyalty to the office or the company. But, you suppose, that's what you must expect these days.

You operate by the rules. They are there for a purpose and there should be no need to deviate from them. You have imposed a system that works well. This is the way that an office should be controlled and organized.

Now that you have got the office running smoothly it is time the company recognized your contribution and you would like a promotion. There are several other places around the company where you think your style and attention to detail would be very useful.

You are about to have your appraisal interview with your manager.

THE FRUSTRATED HIGH FLYER

Role Play 17

Time guide Up to 1½ hours, including time for preparation and review.

Participants 2 plus observers.

Equipment Desk, chairs and tables. (Trainers may wish to provide a choice of formal or informal seating for participants to choose their own preferred setting.)

Copies of the general brief for all participants. Copies of the individual briefs for players of the appraisee and the manager and for the observers.

Notes for role players (Handout 4, page 48) if required. Observers' checklists (for an example see Handout 3, page 47).

Flipchart or whiteboard to record points during the debrief.

Video camera, tripod, recorder and TV monitor (if required).

LEARNING POINTS AND SKILLS PRACTISED

- All the general appraisal skills including questioning, listening, the giving of both positive and negative feedback and the observation of non-verbal signals.
- The exploration of attitudes, perceptions and causes of behaviour.
- The construction of a creative alternative to promotion to maintain interest, motivation and the retention of the employee.
- The firm definition and agreement of plans, targets and objectives.

Procedure See notes on conducting role plays (Checklist, page 49). Brief the participants and allow time for preparation. Meanwhile brief the observers and set up the room to represent the managing director's office. Allow play to continue for up to 30 minutes and then give a few moments for the participants to come out of role before starting the review.

Review See notes on feedback and review in Chapter 2 (Handouts 1 & 2, pages 45 and 46).

In particular, the group should try to answer the following questions as part of the review.

- Was the employee left with a clear impression of how his performance was seen by the managing director?
- Did the man's personal difficulties emerge as cause for recent behaviour change?
- Was an acceptable plan constructed that would give an incentive and a challenge?
- How well did the MD explore all the possible options? How good was his questioning and listening?

HANDOUT
Appraisal – the frustrated high flyer

General brief for all

Ziblab Electronics is a small and highly profitable company working in the field of telecommunications. In particular they have a very high profile in the area of the design and installation of network communications systems.

They have been trading for 6 years, having been founded by the 3 current directors and 3 other technicians who left a large electronics company together to set up Ziblab. The company has now grown to 33 employees. The last year has been much harder than previous years, due largely to increased competition from larger companies in the field who are now catching up with Ziblab's initial technical lead. Profits last year were halved and the company ceased to grow. Current projects will keep the company going for a further year. New contracts are urgently needed; without them there will be no company, let alone any growth.

Three years ago the managing director recruited Norman Dupree, aged 28, who came with high qualifications and 3 years' experience at the forefront of telecommunication systems design. For the last 3 years he has been gradually given more responsibility until, now, he is the senior project manager. His latest contract was for a large slice of the NHS and was completed on time with very few hitches. The fact that it made little money was not his problem. It was, in essence, a case of the initial tender being made too cheap in order to secure the contract.

© David Turner 1992, published by Kogan Page

The organization structure is as follows:

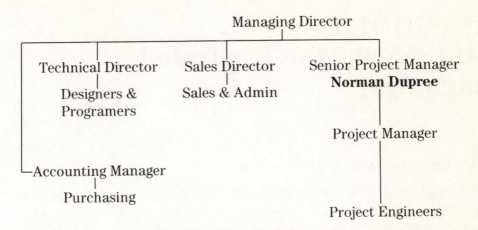

In the project staff there are 17 employees including Norman Dupree. They are all under 35 years of age and are all technically extremely competent.

Both the sales director and the technical director are large stakeholders in the company. They also draw a salary, and are keen to see the company succeed. Growth of the company appears at present to be unlikely, although current negotiations with several prospective clients, if successful, would alter the picture radically.

HANDOUT
Appraisal – the frustrated high flyer

Brief for the managing director

Ziblab was very much your idea and with the other 2 directors you have been delighted with the way things have gone so far. The current situation looks less rosy but it only needs one good contract to emerge from the 7 negotiations that are under way for the way forward to become clear. Competition is strong, however, and getting the margins on contracts is not as easy as it was.

You know that Norman Dupree, your senior project manager, is becoming restless. He is undoubtedly one of the best project managers you have ever met in this business. His technical knowledge and skill is matched with planning and analytical skills and his team works wonders for him. You cannot afford to lose him.

All the projects he managed last year were finished on time, within budget, with so few technical hiccups that the clients were very pleased. Current workloads, however, mean that he is employed on two very small contracts and routine support for existing systems. You know he does not find this a sufficient challenge. You suspect he may be looking elsewhere.

As you approach his appraisal interview you need to decide how to retain him. You cannot help but give him an excellent review, although he has had quite a bit of time off over this last 3 months and he has become very quiet and a bit short-tempered. You suspect he just has not enough to occupy him fully and he is now looking for a more challenging job, hence the time off. You haven't spoken to him before because you have been away a lot and you have only seen him to talk to twice in the last month. Your impression of his changed behaviour comes from the other directors and the odd remark from some of his team.

Obviously, one thing you could do is to get Norman to team up with the sales director, Evan, in order to present a more impressive front to the potential clients. This would give him a change of scene, would strengthen your chances of winning contracts and, hopefully, involve him in the decision-making to the point where he decides to stay. A salary increase at this point is out. In any case, you think it would not be effective, on its own, to retain him. While the other two directors are about there is little chance of a promotion, and both of them are committed to Ziblab anyway. What can you do to tie him in more? Is there something you can do to tie his salary into the performance of the company? Can he buy a stake in the company and would he want to?

HANDOUT
Appraisal – the frustrated high flyer

Brief for the senior project manager

You are Norman Dupree, aged 28. Three years ago you came to Ziblab and for those 3 years you have worked extremely hard and successfully to reach your current position just over a year ago.

You enjoy the challenge of big projects, you thrive on the camaraderie and teamwork when the pressure is on and you have had great success and satisfaction from the major contracts that have now come to an end.

Three months ago, just as the NHS contract was signed off, your wife left you and has filed for divorce. It has become very messy, vindictive and looks as if it will become costly. You have had to take quite some time off lately with solicitors and so on and you know it has been affecting your work recently. You have told no one at work of your problems.

Life has become, suddenly, very different. Until 3 months ago it was great; now there is no wife and the job has become routine and mundane. You need to take your mind off your personal problems but work isn't really doing it for you at the moment.

You are considering an offer from one of your recent clients to go and join them. You haven't thought much about it yet but maybe that would get you away from here into something new. Your preference would be for Ziblab to take off again and you could be heavily involved once more. Even then you cannot see a real career progression here – not unless the MD offered you a chance to take a stake in the business and become a director. You have a little capital left you by your father but, given your domestic and housing situation at present, you might need that for a house. So unless the MD comes up with a deal that does not require you to stump up loads of capital, that idea is probably a pipe dream. Still, no harm in asking!

Chapter 6:

Discipline role plays

The use of disciplinary procedures in the workplace is often regarded by managers as one of the most fraught tasks that they ever have to carry out. Not only are managers forced into taking action which is likely to be unpleasant for the person being disciplined, and possibly unpopular with other members of staff, but they are also operating in areas covered by aspects of employment law about which they may be unclear.

The purpose of a disciplinary procedure is not to punish but to bring about an improvement in performance or adherence to the rules. This can be done informally, in the day to day course of events, or more formally as part of a recognized company procedure. In more formal situations the process is one of investigating facts, setting standards (or the restatement of rules) and defining the future action required. Clearly the consequences of a failure to meet the standards set (and preferably agreed) must be spelt out and a record of the outcome of the interview must be kept.

In any disciplinary interview the facts must be established. The reasons for the poor performance (or failure to comply with the rules) and the degree to which the rules or required standards were understood must be investigated. In fact, the process of the disciplinary interview is very similar to any other interview and the skills of face-to-face communication are all-important.

Thus, role playing disciplinary situations can provide managers with an understanding of the process, give them confidence in their ability to carry it off and enable them to practise the necessary skills.

The particular skills that can be practised include:

- assertiveness;
- questioning and probing for information and feelings;
- listening;
- establishing and agreeing facts;
- summarizing;
- judgement on – the appropriate sanctions within the disciplinary procedure
  - the degree to which assistance is required or appropriate
  - the standards or targets for improvement
  - reliability of evidence and veracity of witnesses;
- control of and dealing with emotion;
- influencing;
- controlling conversations;
- gaining commitment and agreement.

The following scenarios can be used to practise the interviewing skills and to learn the practical application of the organization's disciplinary procedures, whatever they may be.

THE BAD TIMEKEEPER
Role Play 18

Time guide Up to 1½ hours, including 25 minutes for preparation and 30 minutes for review.

Participants 3 or 4 plus observers.(It may be appropriate to have the fourth person, shop steward or friend, to accompany the employee if that is the normal procedure.)

Equipment Desk or table and chairs.

Copies of the briefs for the manager, supervisor and employee (and a second copy of the employee's brief for the shop steward/friend if they are to be present). Copies of all three briefs for the observers.

Notes for role players (Handout 4, page 48) if required.
Observers' checklists (for an example see Handout 3, page 47).

Flipchart or whiteboard to record points from the debrief.

Video camera, tripod, recorder and TV monitor (if required).

LEARNING POINTS AND SKILLS PRACTISED

- All the general interviewing and communication skills including questioning, listening, probing, summarizing and observation of non-verbal signals.
- Defining standards and objectives for future behaviour. Gaining agreement and commitment to them.
- The need to be clear about subsequent events and the consequences of a failure to comply.
- Identifying underlying causes using facts and evidence, not opinion or hearsay.

Procedure See notes on conducting a role play (Checklist, page 49). Brief the participants and allow time for preparation. Meanwhile, brief the observers and arrange the furniture to represent the manager's office. Allow play to continue for up to 30 minutes and then give a little time for players to come out of role and start the review.

Review See notes on feedback and review in Chapter 2 (Handouts 1 & 2, pages 45 and 46).

In particular the group should try to answer the following questions as part of the review.

- What was the manager's attitude? Was it appropriate?
- Did the facts emerge? Did the manager discover reasons for the lateness?
- Was there agreement about the required improvement?
- Were the consequences of a failure to comply made clear?
- Was the outcome fair and reasonable?
- Was there anything else the manager could have done?

HANDOUT
Discipline – the bad timekeeper

Employee's brief

You have been working for the company for 3 years now and you enjoy the work and have had very good reports on the standards that you have achieved. Until 6 months ago you had never had a problem getting to work and you had always been able to get to the office before the start of the normal working day. You are worried about the forthcoming interview with your manager, as you know that she intends to talk to you again about your timekeeping. This job is very important to you and you must keep it to maintain a living wage. Three months ago, when she last spoke to you, she gave you a verbal warning that your timekeeping had to improve to the point where you were late no more than once a month. You know that you have been late at least 7 or 8 times since then and 2 of those occasions have been in this week.

Six months ago your aged mother came to live with you. She is in a wheelchair and requires a great deal of care and attention before you can leave her for the day. You live alone with your mother so you have to do everything for her in the morning. You have managed to arrange a home help who comes in every weekday morning, and you like to speak to her before you leave. You have been getting up very early every morning to deal with all the extra care and chores but, on those days when you have been late for work, you have missed the normal bus because the home help has been late. There is quite a good service, so the next bus gets in only a few minutes later than the one you normally catch, but it does mean that you are about 10 minutes late when that happens. You have been late twice this week because the normal home help is away and there have been two stand-ins who have had to be shown where everything is.

When your manager gave you the warning last time you had not talked about your domestic arrangements and problems since you felt that it was not something you wanted spread about and, anyway, you felt that it might prejudice your chances of promotion if it were known that you had this high level of commitment outside work. You would still like to be considered for promotion, if the opportunity arose, but you know that this timekeeping problem isn't helping and the company do need people who are able to put in extra hours when required. You know that would be difficult for you so you do not want to admit to the problems you have.

Next week, the normal home help should be back and so things should improve. You also think that if you speak to her nicely she might be prepared to get in a few minutes earlier.

HANDOUT
Discipline – the bad timekeeper

Manager's brief

You have asked an employee to come and see you in a few minutes because you want to take further disciplinary action over their timekeeping. This employee has been with the company for about 3 years and their work has always been of a very high standard. However, about 6 months ago, in July, their timekeeping record began to deteriorate and in October you issued a formal verbal warning that this had to stop and that there should be no more than one occasion of being late for work per month in future. You said then that you would continue to monitor their timekeeping for 6 months.

Three months on, you notice that there have been 8 occasions on which they have been late. You have this information from the supervisor who is required to keep a register to help control attendance and timekeeping, as well as to provide details for the payroll. The details are as follows:

Weds	20th Oct	10 mins late
Thurs	28th Oct	15 mins late
Fri	12th Nov	12 mins late
Mon	22nd Nov	8 mins late
Tues	30th Nov	10 mins late
Mon	6th Dec	12 mins late
Tues	11th Jan	15 mins late
Thurs	13th Jan	22 mins late

Today is 14th January, almost exactly 3 months since you issued the verbal warning. On that occasion the employee had been very ready to agree to abide by the standards you set and gave no particular

© David Turner 1992, published by Kogan Page

reason for repeated lateness. You can see no good reason not to progress to the next stage of the disciplinary procedure. You have asked the supervisor of the section to sit in on the interview.

It is a pity, really, that you find yourself having to do this because you had hoped to be able to promote this employee to the next grade because the standard of their work has been good. The next grade is a supervisory grade and you need someone who is reliable, can set a good example over timekeeping and so on, and who would be able to put in extra hours occasionally when necessary. If it goes on like this you certainly won't be able to promote them . . . in fact if your warnings don't work you might be losing them altogether.

HANDOUT
Discipline – the bad timekeeper

Supervisor's brief

One of your staff has developed a bad timekeeping record. They were given a verbal warning by your manager 3 months ago but things do not seem to have improved.

You keep the attendance register for the section which is used for payroll purposes. It also enables you to monitor and control both attendance and timekeeping among your staff. You check the register every month to see if anyone is having excessive time off or if anyone is getting slack about coming in on time.

This morning you did your check after this particular member of staff had come in late and found that, despite the warning 3 months ago that they should not be late more than once a month, they had not improved and in fact seem to be getting worse. Your register reveals lateness as follows:

Wed	20th Oct	10 mins late
Thurs	28th Oct	15 mins late
Fri	12th Nov	12 mins late
Mon	22nd Nov	8 mins late
Tues	30th Nov	10 mins late
Mon	6th Dec	12 mins late
Tues	11th Jan	15 mins late
Thurs	13th Jan	22 mins late

You advised your manager and she has arranged to see the offending employee later and has asked you to sit in.

This particular member of staff has always been very good at the job and you have no complaints. They are not very forthcoming and do not seem to have many friends at work. You know they travel to work by bus from fairly nearby but know of no reason for this poor timekeeping. The only thing you have noticed is that they appear very tired sometimes and recently they have taken to leaving on the dot at the end of the day. Up to about 6 months ago they did seem to be a bit more conscientious and keen to finish the job even if it meant stopping on for a bit.

GROSS MISCONDUCT?

Role Play 19

Time guide Up to 1½ hours, including 20 minutes for preparation and 30 minutes for review.

Participants 4 plus observers

Equipment Desk or table and chairs.

Copies of the general information for all participants.
Copies of the briefs for the manager, foreman, employee and the shop steward/friend. Copies of all 5 briefs for the observers.

Notes for role players (Handout 4, page 48) if required. Observers' checklists (for an example see Handout 3, page 47).

Flipchart or whiteboard to record points from the debrief.

Video camera, tripod, recorder and TV monitor (if required).

LEARNING POINTS AND SKILLS PRACTISED

- All the general interviewing and communication skills, including questioning, listening, probing, summarizing and observation of non-verbal signals.
- Investigation of the facts.
- Ensuring the employee has the chance to put their case.
- The dangers of making snap judgements and the need to make a judgement about who is telling the truth.
- The concepts of fair and unfair dismissal.
- The importance of dealing in facts and evidence, not opinion or hearsay.

© David Turner 1992, published by Kogan Page

Procedure See notes on conducting a role play (Checklist, page 49). Brief the participants and allow time for preparation. Meanwhile, brief the observers and arrange the furniture to represent the manager's office. Allow play to continue for up to 40 minutes and then give a little time for players to come out of role and start the review.

Review See notes on feedback and review in Chapter 2 (Handouts 1 & 2, pages 45 and 46).

In particular the group should try to answer the following questions as part of the review.

- What was the manager's attitude? Was it appropriate?
- How well did the manager establish the facts of the case?
- Was the employee given the chance to put his case?
- Was the action taken appropriate and fair?
- What would be the reaction of the foreman to the outcome?
- Was the procedure to be followed next, or for an appeal, made clear?

HANDOUT
Discipline – gross misconduct?

General information for all

The company you work for, Haulways Transport plc, has been established as a national parcels carrier for several years, with trans-shipment depots in all parts of the country. These depots are where night trunk vehicles' loads are crossdecked (unloaded, sorted to delivery areas and reloaded) by a night shift on to HGV3 delivery vehicles for the next day's deliveries.

At the Herecester depot there is a night shift of 16 who work permanently on nights. They work from midnight to 8 am, 5 nights a week, Monday to Friday. A small shift drawn from the day staff start work early on Monday morning to deal with the reduced volume trunk on Sunday nights. The depot is closed on Saturday night. A fleet of 26 HGV3 vehicles, supplemented if required by sub-contractors, operates daily from the depot. They deliver their loads in the morning and collect parcels for delivery elsewhere during the afternoon. These are returned to the depot, sorted and loaded out on the night trunk vehicles.

The night shift is run by Harry Peterson, an ex-driver, who has been night shift foreman for the last 5 years. The 16 staff have, most of them, been there for several years although there are a few who are recent recruits. The company has never managed to recruit 16 staff who are happy to work permanent nights. There are, therefore, 4 or 5 posts that are constantly turning over with new staff.

On Saturday morning (today is Tuesday), Harry rang the depot manager to say that he had suspended, with pay, one of the shift members and sent him home on suspicion of theft. He has been told to return today for a disciplinary hearing with the depot manager. The man suspended is called Mike Rogers.

© David Turner 1992, published by Kogan Page

The company disciplinary policy states that theft of company property or property of the company's customers is gross misconduct and is likely to result in summary dismissal. A digest of the company's disciplinary policy and rules is issued to all new starters and is occasionally reissued with wage packets as a reminder. The last occasion it was reissued was 6 months ago. The whole policy is available in the general office and a permanent notice is displayed on two notice boards in the depot, drawing attention to its availability to anyone wishing to see it or any of the other company policy statements that are held in the same place.

HANDOUT
Discipline – gross misconduct?

Brief for the depot manager

You are the manager of the Herecester depot of Haulways Transport plc. You have held the post for nearly 3 years. On Saturday morning you were phoned by Harry Peterson, the night shift foreman, to be told that he had suspended one of his men for suspected theft and sent him home on full pay. You heard brief details and agreed that he appeared to have acted correctly.

You have investigated as much as you can, mostly by talking to Harry, but also one or two of the night shift were able to confirm this morning what had happened after Harry had challenged the accused employee, Mike Rogers.

As far as you can determine, Harry came out of the restroom at the end of a break period at about 3.30 am ahead of the rest of the shift. Apparently, Mike Rogers had left the room a few minutes before. Everyone else was in the restroom and began to follow Harry out; Harry tends to signal the end of the break by getting up and leaving. The staff then follow within the next couple of minutes, having packed away flasks and lunch boxes.

As Harry came out on to the loading dock he saw Mike Rogers with his hands in a large parcel that had been ripped open. He asked him what he was doing and he said that he had been trying to repack it. Harry then noticed that Mike had some binoculars sticking up out of his overall pocket. The broken case was found to contain five similar pairs of binoculars and the bent and torn packaging from another pair. The consignment note inside referred to the contents of the box as being 6 pairs of binoculars. Harry concluded that the binoculars in Mike's pocket were the ones missing from the parcel.

Harry was very suspicious and was fairly sure that Mike intended to steal these binos. It was only because he had decided to come out of the restroom in good time (because there was still a lot of work to be done), that he had caught Mike at it. Mike had left the restroom early, Harry thinks, to have the chance to open this box he thought might have contained something valuable.

Mike was told to go to the restroom while Harry considered what to do, and was then sent home, at about 3.45 am, having been told by Harry to be back in on Tuesday for a hearing with you. There had been a few heated words, but Mike had eventually decided to comply, and one of the other men on the shift heard Mike say, 'I'll sort it out on Tuesday. You won't ****** listen, you vindictive old *****!' as he climbed into his car and left.

Mike is comparatively new to the shift, having been taken on 12 weeks ago. He came from the local council's Direct Labour Pool with a perfectly acceptable, if vague, reference. Harry says his work is all right, but his attitude to Harry is a bit ill-mannered and bolshie, and he does need a bit of chasing.

The disciplinary hearing is due to start shortly. You have invited the men's shop steward to attend.

HANDOUT
Discipline – gross misconduct?

Brief for the accused employee

You are Mike Rogers and you have been employed for the last 12 weeks on the night shift at Haulways Transport depot. You came from working for the council, where you had been for the last 12 years, to earn more money by working nights.

You quite like the job and the shift are a likeable bunch of blokes. But the foreman, Harry, gets on your nerves. He never leaves you alone. Every time you straighten your back, it seems that Harry is there telling you to get on with it. You have talked back a few times, accusing Harry of picking on you.

On Friday night, you worked as usual and at about 2 am you went to the toilet. On your return (and you had not been hiding or having a smoke or anything), Harry came up to you and asked you where the hell had you been, and accused you of skiving when you told him. It was another example of Harry's attitude to you.

At the break later you had finished your snack and, having left your newspaper at home, decided to get straight on with loading the van you were on before break. You knew there were plenty more vans to load before the end of the shift and the break was nearly over anyway. As you moved the first trolley to the back of the van a pair of binoculars started to fall out of a damaged box in the pile. They looked a bit unsafe so you stopped, picked them up and put them in your pocket while you lifted the box out of the pile to put it to one side to mend in a moment. You were examining what needed to be done, before fetching the tape dispenser, when Harry came on to the dock and jumped to the conclusion that you had ripped the box and stolen the binoculars.

A few heated words were exchanged, you shouted at him about all the times he had been picking on you for no apparent reason and Harry became all formal and told you to go and cool off in the restroom. The other blokes suggested you had better do as he said and a few minutes later Harry came in, told you to get your things and go home. He said you were suspended on full pay and to come in again today to see the depot manager.

HANDOUT
Discipline – gross misconduct?

Brief for Harry Peterson, the night shift foreman

You have been the night shift foreman for the last 5 years. You run a tight ship and most of the men on the shift have been with you for some time. The turnover among the rest of the shift is quite high and when you get a new employee you like to make sure that they know who is the boss and to make sure they get into the habit of a good night's work.

Your latest member of the shift, Mike Rogers, has been difficult. You have let him know what is required, but he has to have the last word and does not seem to accept that your job as foreman means that you have to supervise what people are doing. You have had words, you and he, a few times. He seems to work reasonably well, but you don't think he really fits in your team.

On Friday as you came out of the restroom after the break you found Mike with his hands in a ripped box and a pair of binoculars in his pocket. He had left the restroom some time before and not returned. You asked him what he was doing and he came up with all sorts of excuses about mending the box. But he had the binos in his pocket, no tape, and you checked that there was a pair missing from the box according to the consignment note on the inside. There was also a damaged package still inside the carton that was empty. Mike must have ripped it to get the binos out.

He started shouting at you, calling you all sorts of things and you decided that now was not the time to start an argument with Mike and sent him off to the restroom. A few minutes later you had decided that the only thing you could do was to suspend him and then the manager would have to deal with it.

The chances are he will have to be sacked. That does not worry you too much, his reaction on Friday night was such that you would find it difficult to work with him again.

The hearing is in the manager's office in a few minutes.

HANDOUT
Discipline – gross misconduct?

Brief for the shop steward

You are the shop steward for the Herecester depot. You work in the warehouse during the day as a fork-lift truck driver.

Mike Rogers is a member of the union and when you spoke to him this morning you gathered that he intends to deny vigorously the accusation of theft raised against him. You don't really know the man, since he works nights.

His story is that he had moved a trolley with this broken parcel and several others on it and as he did so the binoculars had fallen out. He said he had put them in his pocket for safety and extracted the box from the pile so that he could repair it. He would then have returned the binos to it before taping it up again.

According to Mike his foreman, your old friend Harry Peterson, then went off the deep end and jumped to the conclusion that Mike was trying to steal the binoculars. Mike also told you that Harry has had it in for him ever since he arrived to work here 12 weeks ago. An argument followed and Harry told Mike to go home and that he was suspended.

Theft is clearly described in the company's disciplinary policy as gross misconduct, so if Mike was stealing then he will probably be sacked and there is not much you can do about it, but you will do your best to see that he gets a fair hearing and that there should be good reason to dismiss him if that is what is decided.

The depot manager has always been fair and you have never had to challenge a disciplinary decision before. This is, however, the first time that you have been involved in a case of gross misconduct with summary dismissal as the likely outcome.

THE BAD BACK
Role Play 20

Time guide Up to 1½ hours, including 30 minutes for preparation and 30 minutes for review.

Participants 2 plus observers.

Equipment Desk or table and chairs.

A copy of the general brief for both players. Copies of the briefs for the managing director and employee. Copies of all 3 briefs for the observers.

Notes for role players (Handout 4, page 48) if required. Observers' checklists (for an example see Handout 3, page 47).

Flipchart or whiteboard to record points from the debrief.

Video camera, tripod, recorder and TV monitor (if required).

LEARNING POINTS AND SKILLS PRACTISED

- All the general interviewing and communication skills including questioning, listening, probing, summarizing and observation of non-verbal signals.
- Identification of the cause of the problem being addressed and establishing facts.
- Defining standards and objectives for future behaviour. The need to separate the sickness from the absence.
- The need to be clear about subsequent events and the consequences of a failure to improve.
- The need to find creative solutions to achieve the desired results.
- The need for fair and reasonable behaviour by the employer.

Procedure See notes on conducting a role play (Checklist, page 49). Brief the participants and allow time for preparation. Meanwhile brief the observers and arrange the furniture to represent the managing director's office. Allow play to continue for up to 40 minutes and then give a little time for players to come out of role and start the review.

Review See notes on feedback and review in Chapter 2 (Handouts 1 & 2, pages 45 and 46).

In particular the group should try to answer the following questions as part of the review.

- What was the managing director's attitude? Was it appropriate? What should it have been?
- How well were the facts established?
- Was the outcome appropriate and fair?
- Were the consequences of a failure to improve made clear?
- Was a disciplinary approach the right one in this case?

HANDOUT
Discipline – the bad back

General information for all

Softgame Ltd employs about 30 people and they are involved in the production of computer games software.

Most of the employees are young and employed in the design and production sections. There is a small despatch section of 3 who pack and despatch orders received.

The work at Softgame is varied, exciting and very pressurized. It is a young company and pay and benefits are excellent. One feature is a company sick scheme that is designed to make up the difference between statutory sick pay and normal earnings and pay a reduced rate for sickness absence for a further 130 days in any one year. The payment of this benefit is at the discretion of the managing director, whose company it is.

John Harris is the oldest employee at 52 and last year he had an accident at work which left him laid up for a long time. He has returned to work on 3 or 4 occasions in the last 4 months but only to find the job too stressful on his weakened back.

HANDOUT
Discipline – the bad back

Brief for the managing director

You have set up and run this company for the last 4 years. It has been extremely profitable and you have tried to put some of the rewards in the direction of the people that work for you. For that reason, salaries and benefits are very good. You do expect your staff to work hard for it.

Just recently sales have started to decline and the latest product is not doing well. You are going to have to cut costs until things pick up.

You have one employee, John Harris, who is currently off sick with a bad back. He works in the despatch section which is predominantly a manual job. In fact the injury was caused by an accident at work. That was about 18 months ago and has all been sorted out, but you still see very little of him. His statutory sick pay was exhausted a long time ago and you have agreed to go on paying him, at the reduced rate, for his absences so far. He has now been paid for 100 days under the company sick scheme.

In the last 9 months he has only put in 12 weeks' work. Each time he comes back it is only a matter of a few days or a week or two before he is off again saying his back's gone again. This means that you have had to employ temps to cover his absence and, of course, continue to pay his sick pay.

You need to get him back to work on a permanent basis. You are not getting your money's worth out of this man.

There is a vacancy for a driver cum handyman cum gardener (no digging involved) but you wouldn't want to pay the same rate for that job as for despatch work. If John took the job he would be worse off by about £35 a week compared to his normal wage when working.

You have arranged to see John in a few minutes to try and put the situation right.

HANDOUT
Discipline – the bad back

Brief for John Harris

You have worked for Softgame ever since it started. You have been doing the despatches throughout, at first on your own and then with help.

Eighteen months ago you hurt your back lifting some cartons of diskettes into a van and it hasn't been right since. You want to get back to work not only because you are bored at home all day but also because the money is good (you are very grateful for the way the MD has agreed to carry on paying you something while you are off). Apart from which, they have been good to you and you don't want to let them down.

Every time you return, however, your back goes again and that means another week or two virtually laid up. Your doctor is not very optimistic about your back ever being very strong.

You suspect that the boss is going to tell you that he can't go on paying you like this and you are very worried that he might be planning to sack you.

You are due to see him in a few minutes.

THE POOR PERFORMER
Role Play 21

Time guide Up to 1 hour, including 20 minutes for preparation and 20 minutes for review.

Participants 2 plus observers.

Equipment Desk or table and chairs.

Copies of the general brief for everyone and copies of the briefs for the manager and the employee. Copies of all 3 briefs for the observers.

Notes for role players (Handout 4, page 48) if required. Observers' checklists (for an example see Handout 3, page 47).

Flipchart or whiteboard to record points from the debrief.

Video camera, tripod, recorder and TV monitor (if required).

LEARNING POINTS AND SKILLS PRACTISED

- All the general interviewing and communication skills including questioning, listening, probing, summarizing and observation of non-verbal signals.
- The importance of establishing the facts and identifying the cause of the problem being addressed.
- Defining standards and objectives for future performance.
- The need to be clear about subsequent events and the consequences of a failure to improve.
- The need for fair and reasonable behaviour by the employer.

Procedure See notes for the conduct of role plays (Checklist, page 49). Brief the participants and allow time for preparation. Meanwhile brief the observers and arrange the furniture to represent the manager's office. Allow play to continue for up to 20 minutes and then give a little time for players to come out of role and start the review.

Review See notes on feedback and review in Chapter 2 (Handouts 1 & 2, page 45 and 46).

In particular, the group should try to answer the following questions as part of the review.

- What was the manager's attitude? Was it appropriate?
- Were the facts made clear?
- Were the standards required clearly defined?
- Was the outcome fair and reasonable?
- Were the consequences of a failure to improve clearly stated?
- Did the employee understand the need to improve?
- What other options were open to the manager?

HANDOUT
Discipline – the poor performer

General brief for all

The fulfilment (order processing) department of this large mail order organization employs over 150 people. This number of people are required to operate VDUs to update customer records, enter orders, answer correspondence and process cash/cheques received by mail.

The prestige section in the department is the correspondence section and it is about 50 strong. Its staff are on higher grades than the rest of the department owing to the range and complexities of the tasks to be carried out and their direct impact on the customer. Trainees in their first 3 months start on a basic wage the same as other staff elsewhere in the department. Their grade is changed, up one, after the 3-month probationary period. There are a further 3 more senior clerical grades for clerks to aim for. They are awarded on the basis of both expertise and consistent output.

The section has its own induction and training routine. It normally takes about 3 weeks before the new employee can be left to get on with simple work and then all their output is monitored regularly until a consistent standard is maintained. Gradually new modules and tasks are added with the same training and monitoring process.

The normal standards for the first level of correspondence clerk are:

- a daily output, averaged over a month, of 75 replies to queries and the necessary transactions on the customer account completed;
- an accuracy level of 94 per cent in terms of both numerical accuracy and correctness of actions taken/transactions made.

This accuracy is monitored by a routine inspection of totals and an occasional but regular checking of the individual's actual output. For trainees or those with problems this monitoring can cover up to 30 per cent of their output. This is very time consuming for supervisors and every attempt is made to ensure that staff reach an acceptable standard quickly.

HANDOUT
Discipline – the poor performer

Brief for the manager

You are the manager of the fulfilment department. One operator who was recruited as a trainee correspondence clerk has been consistently failing to reach the required standards of output and quality. When recruited, 6 months ago, the standard training programme was started with the regular trainer from the department. This particular employee took much longer than average to achieve the required basic standard. At the end of the normal 3-month probationary period, however, the supervisor and the trainer were of the opinion that it was a case of a slow learner and employment was confirmed. Since then there has been very little evidence of any real progress in terms of accuracy although the level of output has reached satisfactory levels.

In this case, despite repeated monitoring and much coaching by the trainer, an accuracy level of 94 per cent has never been achieved. In fact the best to date has been 87 per cent. The regular average result is only 82 per cent accuracy. The problem appears to be one of careless mistakes. Generally the types of transactions to customers' accounts seem to have been appropriate to the circumstances and the laid down guidelines. However, transcription, addition and typographical errors are frequent and account for most of the poor results from the supervisor's monitoring exercise.

The time has come to ascertain whether there is a problem for this individual or whether the job is beyond them. The need is for competent and consistently accurate operators and the standards are well defined. You want to ensure that this individual knows precisely what standard is required and what the consequences are of a failure to achieve them. You are due to see them shortly.

This will be the first time that any formal action will have been taken. There are other jobs of a more routine clerical nature that this person could be transferred to, but the grades in those jobs are lower and so is the pay (by about £20 per week).

HANDOUT
Discipline – the poor performer

Brief for the correspondence clerk

You came to work here 6 months ago in the correspondence section. The work is quite varied and interesting. You enjoy having to decide how to resolve customers' problems and complaints and you have to admit that the system with which you work to update customers' accounts and generate letters is excellent.

There is an awful lot to learn. It took you several weeks to understand all that was going on within the company and within the office, let alone all the complexities of the job itself. Your supervisor and the trainer have been very patient. You know that you have taken longer than they expected to become proficient with the basic system and the most common range of transactions. At last you believe you have got it. Your output totals have reached the required numbers some time ago. You make a few mistakes, mostly silly ones. You are sure it is because you are concentrating (and worrying) so much about what actions to take that the silly errors creep in.

Your supervisor has spoken to you a couple of times about accuracy and some percentage figure or other, but you have been unlucky that all your mistakes happened to be in the batches of work examined.

The office is a good one to work in and it is nice to work with your great friend from school; your VDUs are next door to each other so you get a chance to chat quietly while you work. The prospect of further grade increases and higher wages appeals a lot. You think you could really get to like it here.

Your manager has asked to see you about your performance. You imagine it is to say that she is pleased that at last you are achieving the output totals.

THE SECOND OFFENCE
Role Play 22

Time guide Up to 1½ hours, including 30 minutes for preparation and 30 minutes for review.

Participants 4 plus observers.

Equipment Desk or table and chairs.

Copies of the briefs for the manager, employee, loading-bay supervisor and shop steward. Copies of all 4 briefs for the observers. Copies of the written warning letter for all.

Notes for role players (Handout 4, page 48) if required. Observers' checklists (for an example see Handout 3, page 47).

Flipchart or whiteboard to record points from the debrief.

Video camera, tripod, recorder and TV monitor (if required).

LEARNING POINTS AND SKILLS PRACTISED

- All the general interviewing and communication skills including questioning, listening, probing, summarizing and observation of non-verbal signals.
- The importance of establishing the facts and identifying the cause of the problem being addressed.
- Reviewing previous disciplinary actions and the consequences of a failure to comply.
- Defining standards and targets for future performance.
- The need to be clear about subsequent events and the consequences of a failure to comply with the rules.

Procedure See notes on conducting a role play (Checklist, page 49). Brief the participants and allow time for preparation. Meanwhile brief the observers and arrange the furniture to represent the manager's office. Allow play to continue for up to 30 minutes and then give a little time for players to come out of role and start the review.

Review See notes on feedback and review in Chapter 2 (Handouts 1 & 2, pages 45 and 46).

In particular, the group should try to answer the following questions as part of the review.

- What was the manager's attitude? Was it appropriate?
- Were the facts clearly established?
- Was the employee given a fair hearing?
- Were the rules clearly stated and understood?
- Was the action taken fair and reasonable?
- Should or could the manager do anything to help this employee?

HANDOUT
Discipline – the second offence

Copy of the letter issued on 12th September 1992 to Mr Arthur Kemp, warehouseman, by the distribution manager.

WINSLOW WIDGETS plc
17 Hardwick Drive
Keyturn Industrial Estate
WINSLOW
Huntfordshire
AF17 4GS

Mr A Kemp
27 Chancelor Grove
WINSLOW
Huntfordshire
AF17 9BY

12 September 1992

Dear Mr Kemp

Three months ago, on the 10th June 1992, I spoke to you about your persistent failure to observe the no smoking rule in the warehouse. At that time I reminded you that smoking on the warehouse floor was something that the company could not accept. Not only is smoking a potential safety hazard, it is also a habit which some staff find unpleasant. Also at that time I informed you, informally, that were you to be found smoking on the premises anywhere other than in one of the two smokers' restrooms further disciplinary action might result.

Yesterday, your supervisor informed me that she had found you smoking in the rear of a lorry at the loading dock. A formal disciplinary meeting was held yesterday afternoon. You were unable to provide any excuse for your action, which you admitted.

This letter is confirmation of the action that I took at that meeting, namely to issue a formal warning that if, within the next 6 months, you are found smoking in the warehouse where it is not permitted you will be given a final warning which, if ignored, would result in your dismissal.

If you are unhappy with the disciplinary action taken against you, you may appeal in writing to the Operations Director, giving your reasons.

Yours sincerely

Distribution manager

Copy to Personnel

HANDOUT
Discipline – the second offence

Brief for the distribution manager

You are the distribution manager for Winslow Widgets plc. Two months ago you issued a written warning to Arthur Kemp for smoking in the warehouse. Smoking was banned on the site following a fire inspection by the local authority fire safety team in which some criticism had been levelled at the company. Smoking was not specifically a problem for the warehouse in the report; only in the packaging store was it seen as a problem. Given quite a loud lobby among the workforce to ban it anyway, it was felt advisable to impose the ban after consultation with the union last year. Specific rest areas for smokers are designated around the warehouse and factory site.

This morning the loading bay supervisor, Arthur Kemp's immediate boss, came to see you to tell you that she'd found Arthur smoking again. This time he was hiding behind a stack of pallets where there is little traffic. Apparently he'd been supposed to be assembling the next export load, due for collection tomorrow. You told the supervisor that there had better be a disciplinary hearing and arranged for the meeting to be held in a few minutes' time. You have also invited the shop steward to attend. From Arthur's file you have recovered the copy of the warning that you gave him.

© David Turner 1992, published by Kogan Page

HANDOUT
Discipline – the second offence

Brief for the offending employee

You are Arthur Kemp, aged 52, and you have worked in the warehouse of Winslow Widgets for 12 years. Last year the company banned smoking in the warehouse and the factory saying it was something to do with fire precautions. You have always been a heavy smoker and for years there was never any problem about having a cigarette while you worked. Now, except at break times, you cannot smoke at all. You can't go for the 2- or 3-hour periods between breaks without a smoke. The company takes a dim view of smoking in the toilets and there is no alternative for you but to grab a smoke when you can.

This morning you were having a cigarette behind a pile of pallets when up comes your supervisor and tells you off for smoking again. She said she was going to report you to the distribution manager, her boss. Later she told you to be outside the manager's office a few minutes from now. You are now waiting to be called in. Your shop steward, who has also been asked along, is with you.

You were given a hard time by the manager a few weeks ago over a similar incident, when you were warned not to do it again and given some letter to prove the warning.

You were not causing a problem for the supervisor over work. The export load you were assembling is not due out until tomorrow and, in fact, it is finished already. You completed it an hour ago.

You are annoyed about this smoking business. Why shouldn't you have a smoke when you need one?

HANDOUT
Discipline – the second offence

Brief for the loading bay supervisor

You are the loading bay supervisor for Winslow Widgets. One of your crew, Arthur Kemp, is an inveterate smoker. The company banned smoking last year, after consultation with the union and after some criticisms by the Fire Service. Since then Arthur has been a real nuisance.

He keeps disappearing, presumably for a smoke, outside break times, and you often can't find him when you want to. He's a crafty so-and-so and he must have several little hideouts for a quick smoke. You caught him at it in the back of a lorry a few weeks ago and this resulted in his being given a formal warning, confirmed in writing, that he should not smoke in the warehouse.

This morning you smelt tobacco in a quiet part of the warehouse where you had been to check some stock and there was Arthur, cigarette in hand. You told him off and reported him to the distribution manager, who has arranged a disciplinary hearing for a few minutes' time.

HANDOUT
Discipline – the second offence

Brief for the shop steward

You are the warehouse shop steward for Winslow Widgets. You were closely involved last year in the company's decision to ban smoking on the premises. They consulted you and your colleagues at that time and the majority of your union members were in favour of the ban. Apparently, the local Fire Service had also been critical of smoking in the packaging store and the company had taken it to heart and decided to do something about smoking in general. Personally, you are very pleased about the ban. You have never smoked and dislike the habit intensely. Arthur Kemp, one of your members, is a heavy smoker whom you have been advising for months to watch his step, since he keeps disappearing for a cigarette. Now the silly fool has been caught by his supervisor lighting up behind a pile of pallets at the back of the warehouse and there is going to be a disciplinary hearing with the distribution manager.

Only two months ago Arthur was given a written warning for smoking and now it looks as if he's bound to get another one. You also do not want to see him get a final warning, which could happen. You will try and get the action reduced to another formal warning. You suppose you had better stress the man's hard work and addiction to nicotine and this being a temporary lapse.

© David Turner 1992, published by Kogan Page

THE CHRISTMAS LUNCH

Role Play 23

Time guide Up to 1½ hours, including time for preparation and review. (Could be 15 to 20 minutes longer if the manager elects to hold 2 interviews).

Participants 4 plus observers.

Equipment Desk or table and chairs.

Copies of the briefs for the manager, supervisor, employee and shop steward. Copies of all 4 briefs for the observers.

Notes for role players (Handout 4, page 48) if required. Observers' checklists (for an example see Handout 3, page 47).

Flipchart or whiteboard to record points from the debrief.

Video camera, tripod, recorder and TV monitor (if required).

LEARNING POINTS AND SKILLS PRACTISED

- All the general interviewing and communication skills including questioning, listening, probing, summarizing and observation of non-verbal signals.
- The dangers of making snap judgements and the need, sometimes, to make a judgement about who is telling the truth.
- Disciplinary rights and procedures. Whatever the procedures within the organization are, they should be applied here.
- The importance of dealing in facts and evidence, not opinion or hearsay.

Procedure See notes on conducting a role play (Checklist, page 49). Brief the participants and allow time for preparation. Meanwhile brief the observers and arrange the furniture to represent the manager's office. Allow play to continue for up to 30 minutes and then give a little time for players to come out of role and start the review.

The manager must decide how to approach this incident. If it is felt that there may be a case for the supervisor also to be disciplined, two interviews may be required.

Review See notes on feedback and review in Chapter 2 (Handouts 1 & 2, pages 45 and 46).

In particular, the group should try to answer the following questions:

- Was the manager's approach the most effective one? Did he have an open mind on the issue? What was his approach to the supervisor's actions?
- Did the true facts emerge?
- Was the action taken fair and reasonable?
- How would the supervisor react to what was done?
- Is 'blame' a concept for disciplinary interviews?

HANDOUT
Discipline – the Christmas lunch

Brief for the factory manager

You are the factory manager at this furniture factory. Every Christmas, a few days before the factory closes for a short break, the company arranges and subsidizes a turkey lunch with all the trimmings in the staff restaurant for all those staff who wish to attend. Take-up is pretty good and most people go. There is usually a live disco, a glass of wine for everyone (at other times alcohol is strictly forbidden on the premises) and an extra 40 minutes is added to the lunch break that day. In fact, there are so many people wanting to go that they will not all fit in the restaurant at one sitting so the lunch happens twice, on consecutive days.

Yesterday you attended the lunch and it appeared to have gone well. The disco started up for its 30 to 40 minute session and you decided to leave. As the lunch finished your assistant manager came to you to say that there had been a bit of a scrap between a section supervisor and one of his staff. It appears that words were exchanged, although no one else actually heard what was said, and the employee swung a punch at the supervisor. At that point some other members of the section intervened and pulled them apart. You went down to the section, found both men there smelling strongly of drink and the supervisor with a cut lip. You sent them both home and told them to report back this morning to see you.

They are about to come and see you. Do you wish to see them together or separately?

HANDOUT
Discipline – the Christmas lunch

Brief for the supervisor

You are the supervisor of one of the sections in this furniture factory. Every Christmas, a few days before the factory closes for a short break, the company arranges and subsidizes a turkey lunch with all the trimmings in the staff restaurant for all those staff who wish to attend. Take-up is pretty good and most people go. There is usually a live disco, a glass of wine for everyone and an extra 40 minutes is added to the lunch break that day. In fact, there are so many people wanting to go that they will not all fit in the restaurant at one sitting so the lunch happens twice, on consecutive days.

You managed to persuade your whole section of 12 men to attend this lunch yesterday and you all sat together until the end of the meal. Then the disco started up and most of the lads drifted off to dance. The girls from the soft furnishing section were having a great time dancing. You and one of your men sat there chatting and finishing off the wine that the company had provided and the two bottles that you always bring in for the lads for the lunch. Alcohol is strictly forbidden on the premises at all other times, but with the company providing a bit for everyone for the Christmas lunch, you and some of the other supervisors have taken to smuggling in a little bit extra. This time no one had drunk much and the two of you got through several glasses each before it was time to return to work. The conversation had been very general until you got on to the subject of fork-lift truck driving – this chap is your fork-lift truck driver. He has become very quiet lately, distracted somehow and not concentrating on the job. You don't think much of his driving, which has got worse in the last few weeks and you made some remark about him being an accident waiting to happen.

At that point he got up and took a swing at you, catching you across the mouth, drawing blood. Some lads from your section pulled you apart and marched you both off to the section. You don't want to make a big thing of this. If the chap gets a warning and is told to keep his fists to himself, you'll be happy with that. You were a bit surprised that the manager sent you both home but you suppose he had to be seen to be impartial until the facts became clear. It was strange how this bloke reacted to your remarks in this way, though.

HANDOUT
Discipline – the Christmas lunch

Brief for the fork-lift truck driver

You drive a fork-lift truck in one of the sections of this furniture factory. Every Christmas, a few days before the factory closes for a short break, the company arranges and subsidizes a turkey lunch with all the trimmings in the staff restaurant for all those staff who wish to attend. Take-up is pretty good and most people go. There is usually a live disco, a glass of wine for everyone and an extra 40 minutes is added to the lunch break that day. In fact, there are so many people wanting to go that they will not all fit in the restaurant at one sitting so the lunch happens twice, on consecutive days.

You went to the lunch yesterday unwillingly and only because the rest of the lads were keen to go. For the last 4 weeks you have been totally absorbed with an accident that happened to you one evening on your way home from visiting your aged mother in a home. A child had run out between two parked cars in a dark lane and you had no chance. You hit the child. You weren't travelling very fast so the child was not killed, but 4 weeks later she is still in a coma in hospital and there is no indication of when or whether she will regain consciousness. It haunts you terribly. You have not spoken to anyone about this at work but you have to accept that it has affected you and your work. You can't concentrate somehow.

At the lunch, after the meal, you were chatting to your supervisor and drinking some wine he had brought. You were probably knocking it back a bit too quickly, but when he started criticizing your driving and made some remark about an accident, you saw red. You hit him. He just doesn't know the stress your accident has put you under. Straight after you had hit him a couple of the lads pulled you apart and took you off separately to the section. Hitting him was a stupid thing to do. He's not a bad bloke really. You want to apologize to him today.

The manager came down, sent you home and told you to come back today. You are about to see him.

HANDOUT
Discipline – the Christmas lunch

Brief for the shop steward

Every Christmas, a few days before your furniture factory closes for a short break, the company arranges and subsidizes a turkey lunch with all the trimmings in the staff restaurant for all those staff who wish to attend. Take-up is pretty good and most people go. There is usually a live disco, a glass of wine for everyone and an extra 40 minutes is added to the lunch break that day. In fact, there are so many people wanting to go that they will not all fit in the restaurant at one sitting so the lunch happens twice, on consecutive days.

After yesterday's lunch (you attended the lunch the previous day), the manager called you to tell you that he had suspended a supervisor and a fork-lift truck driver from his section after a fight at the lunch. You have had a chat with the lads on the section but, apart from the fact that there had been a short argument and a punch thrown, they are unable to shed any more light on the incident.

Alcohol is usually forbidden in the factory but supervisors have traditionally turned a blind eye to the rule on the day of the Christmas lunch. You understand that both of the men had a fair bit during and after the meal. You have been asked to attend the interview that the manager is about to have with the two men involved.

ACCIDENT-PRONE OR CARELESS?

Role Play 24

Time guide Up to 1¼ hours, including time for preparation and review.

Participants 2 plus observers. (Additional participants may be included to represent a supervisor or union representative if required.)

Equipment Desk or table and chairs.

Copies of the briefs for the manager and the employee. Copies of both briefs for the observers. Appropriate briefs for additional players if present.

Notes for role players (Handout 4, page 48) if required. Observers' checklists (for an example see Handout 3, page 47).

Flipchart or whiteboard to record points from the debrief.

Video camera, tripod, recorder and TV monitor (if required).

LEARNING POINTS AND SKILLS PRACTISED

- All the general interviewing and communication skills including questioning, listening, probing, summarizing and observation of non-verbal signals.
- The importance of establishing the facts and identifying the cause of the problem being addressed.
- Gaining acceptance of a need to improve.
- Defining standards and targets for future performance. Assessing the need for extra training.
- The need to be clear about subsequent events and the consequences of a failure to comply with the rules.

© David Turner 1992, published by Kogan Page

Procedure See notes on conducting a role play (Checklist, page 49). Brief the participants and allow time for preparation. Meanwhile brief the observers and arrange the furniture to represent the manager's office. Allow play to continue for up to 30 minutes and then give a little time for players to come out of role and start the review.

Review See notes on feedback and review in Chapter 2 (Handouts 1 & 2, pages 45 and 46).

In particular, the group should try to answer the following questions as part of the review.

- Were the facts clearly established?
- Was the employee given a fair hearing? Was the employee given a chance to explain the record of accidents?
- Were the requirements for the future clearly stated and understood?
- Was the action taken fair and reasonable? What sanctions could the manager use if there is a failure to improve?

HANDOUT
Discipline – accident-prone or careless?

Brief for the manager

You are the manager of the finished goods store for the Tumbler Toys factory. You employ a small staff whose task it is to store, assemble, select, pack and despatch goods from the factory to your distribution agents around the country and abroad.

The goods are collected on pallets from the ends of the production lines and delivered to the finished goods store by your fork-lift trucks. You have 4 of these with 4 regular drivers and a stand-in for holidays and sickness. These truck drivers operate sophisticated machines in your high-rise, narrow-aisle store and are paid a premium of £30 per week above the standard wage. They are 'qualified' by a company 'licence' issued once they have passed a course run by the truck manufacturer. There is a waiting list of employees who have expressed the wish to become fork-lift truck drivers.

One of your drivers, who was given your 'licence' about 18 months ago, has had a string of minor accidents; a pallet dropped here, a fork through a carton there and at least two occasions where the truck has emerged from the aisle and failed to stop before hitting the wall. Not only has stock been damaged but so too has the truck. Last time the cost of repairs reached £350 and the truck was unavailable for 3 days.

Yesterday there was another accident involving this driver. This time, as the truck came through the draught curtains between factory and store, a passing worker was knocked to the floor by the pallet of cartons that was being carried. Fortunately, the victim was not seriously hurt, suffering only a bruised leg and a grazed hand.

This happened just before the end of work and your store supervisor arranged to speak to the driver this morning. This he did, as well as finding out from the accident victim and another witness as much as possible about what happened. He then came to see you, told you what he understood events to have been and it was agreed to have the driver in for a disciplinary interview.

Apparently the accident happened beside the draught curtains which are opaque. There is a well-understood rule that drivers passing through these curtains should sound the horn and then proceed very slowly until they have a clear view past the curtains. The horn was not sounded. In addition it is normal safe practice on these trucks to drive with the driver leading, particularly when working in areas outside the aisles, in restricted visibility and with a large or heavy load up. In this case the pallet came through the curtain first – the driver cannot have been able to see properly – at a very fast speed. The victim, who was passing the curtains, was unable to leap out of the way of the pallet in time.

It appears that the driver was driving unsafely and in contravention of the rules and of normal safe practice. Your interview with the driver is due to start in a few minutes.

HANDOUT
Discipline – accident-prone or careless?

Brief for the fork-lift truck driver

You have been a fork-lift truck driver in the finished goods store at Tumbler Toys factory for 18 months. You qualified as a truck driver in the way that is standard in the company, by taking and passing the course run by the manufacturers of the truck that you drive. This entitled you to a company 'licence'. The trucks are large, complex machines with a 10-metre lift, rotating forks and a rising cab for operating in the store's narrow aisles. You are one of 4 regular drivers paid a £30 weekly premium above the standard wage. The job is much sought after.

One part of the job entails moving out of the store into the factory to collect pallets of finished materials from the end of production lines. It is only a short journey but, you believe, a dangerous one. It would be better if they could be brought through the doorway for you.

A year ago the factory staff complained of cold draughts when the store doors were open to load goods out on to vehicles. The solution was the insertion of some opaque strip curtains in the doorway. The truck drivers voiced their concern at the time about lack of visibility but were overruled because there was already a rule that drivers should sound their horn when passing through doorways and proceed slowly whenever they were moving outside the storage aisles (which are prohibited to pedestrians). A further safety instruction from the company requires drivers to proceed 'driver first' for the sake of visibility.

Both these rules are pretty daft. First, the amount of work that you and your truck are required to do means that travelling slowly is impossible. Second, travelling 'driver first' is also silly since by raising the cab a little you can see over any load and there just isn't time to turn the truck around all the time.

Yesterday evening you were coming through the strip curtain, as usual, only to find that the pallet on the forks in front of you had knocked over one of the storemen. This only goes to prove how dangerous that doorway is with the curtains. You didn't see him. Fortunately he wasn't badly hurt and is back at work this morning. He seemed distinctly frosty to you, but it is a problem with that doorway. Your supervisor spoke to you about it this morning and you told him again all about the dangers and difficulties you face. He seemed more concerned about rules and procedures and told you later that you were to see the boss for some disciplinary thing.

You want to make sure that the boss understands the problem and does something about it. You will not accept that the accident was your fault. You have a fairly good driving record. There have only been a few minor accidents causing a little damage to stock. Oh yes, there was one when you came out of an aisle too fast and crashed into the wall and bent the rotation mechanism and dislodged some bricks. You had better keep quiet about that one.

You are due to see the boss in a few minutes.

FAILURE TO MEET TARGETS

Role Play 25

Time guide Up to 1½ hours, including time for preparation review.

Participants 2 plus observers.

Equipment Desk or table and chairs.

Copies of the general brief for all. Copies of the briefs for the manager and the employee. Copies of both briefs for the observers.

Notes for role players (Handout 4, page 48) if required. Observers' checklists (for an example see Handout 3, page 47).

Flipchart or whiteboard to record points from the debrief.

Video camera, tripod, recorder and TV monitor (if required).

LEARNING POINTS AND SKILLS PRACTISED

- All the general interviewing and communication skills including questioning, listening, probing, summarizing and observation of non-verbal signals.
- The importance of establishing the facts and identifying the cause of the problem being addressed.
- Gaining acceptance of the need to improve.
- Defining standards and targets for future performance. Assessing the need for extra training.
- The need to be clear about subsequent events and the consequences of a failure to achieve results.

Procedure See notes on conducting a role play (Checklist, page 49). Brief the participants and allow time for preparation. Meanwhile brief the observers and arrange the furniture to represent the manager's office. Allow play to continue for up to 30 minutes and then give a little time for players to come out of role and start the review.

Review See notes on feedback and review in Chapter 2 (Handouts 1 & 2, pages 45 and 46).

In particular, the group should try to answer the following questions as part of the review.

- Were the facts clearly established?
- Was the employee given a fair hearing? Was the employee given a chance to explain his low level of sales?
- Were the requirements for the future clearly stated and understood?
- Was the action taken fair and reasonable? What sanctions could the manager use if there is a failure to improve?
- Is there any help that the manager could give?

HANDOUT
Discipline – failure to meet targets

General brief for all

Smallsorts Confectionery plc is one of 2 or 3 market leaders in non-chocolate confectionery in the country.

The sales force is organized by region, area and territory. Regional and area sales managers have personal responsibility for the national and major accounts whose head offices are in their areas and the area sales managers have a number of territory reps reporting to them covering other outlets. These are mainly CTNs (confectioners, tobacconists and newsagents) although there are some larger independent retailers, cash and carrys and wholesalers who are dealt with by the appropriate territory reps.

The reps are paid a good basic salary, plus a bonus annually that is based on their performance against set targets and a flat rate bonus of £150 for every new customer they sign up.

The annual bonus this year will be 3 per cent of any sales above target. Reps also have a company car and phone bills paid for by Smallsorts. There are various competitions for reps and area managers with significant cash bonuses or prizes for the winners.

Annual sales targets are set by area managers in conjunction with individual reps after long and detailed discussions about their customers, their prospects and their list of potential clients. The targets, when set, should eventually reflect what the company requires, what regional and area managers expect and what the reps themselves believe is possible.

HANDOUT
Discipline – failure to meet targets

Brief for the sales manager

You are the area sales manager for Smallsorts Confectionery plc.

You have managed, quite comfortably, to meet your area sales targets for the last 4 years, despite annual increases. All, bar one, of your reps have also more or less met their targets for their territories.

Last year you thought you were in with a chance of winning the area trophy for the largest increase in sales but came a close second. This was due to the failure of one territory to come up to expectations.

The rep who failed last year has also not performed well for the first 6 months of this year. He has failed to meet agreed targets even though he has what ought to be the most profitable territory in your area. This territory has the highest number of CTNs as well as several very active cash and carrys.

You agreed a sales target of £220,000 this year, April to April, of which £90,000 should be achieved in the first 6 months. So far his sales have reached a very disappointing £45,000. Last year he was £30,000 below target (16 per cent). The sales he has achieved seem to reflect the same product mix as in other territories but the level of sales to CTNs is very poor. This sector should represent some 40 per cent of the total for the patch. At present these sales total only £10,000. In his favour, he has introduced several new customers from non-traditional sectors (garden centres, works canteens, DIY stores, etc).

You have obviously been aware of the poor performance for some time and have spent a great deal of time with him. You have discussed his techniques, call rates, etc and you have accompanied him on his rounds about twice a month for the last 6 months. He seems to perform very well when you are about. This is borne out by the new customers he has signed up. The only thing to which you can attribute his poor performance is that he is perhaps failing to call on all his customers as often as he should. If that is the case, he is falsifying his daily records of calls made, etc.

The time has come to try and find out what the problem is, and to leave him with the clear message that he must improve, or else . . .

You have called him to your office. He is due in a few minutes.

HANDOUT
Discipline – failure to meet targets

Brief for the territory salesman

You are a sales rep for Smallsorts Confectionery plc. You have a large territory with lots of potential for new customers. In fact you have earned over £3000 from bonuses for opening new accounts. This has helped to make up for the poor results from your CTN customers.

You agreed, with your area manager, a sales target of £220,000 this year, April to April, of which £90,000 was to have been achieved in the first 6 months. So far your sales have reached £45,000. Last year you were £30,000 below target (16 per cent). The sales you have achieved seem to reflect the same product mix as in other territories but the level of sales to CTNs is very poor. This sector should represent some 40 per cent of the total for the patch. So far this year these sales total only £10,000 but, if you were honest, you wouldn't expect any more. However, in your favour, you have introduced several new customers from non-traditional sectors (garden centres, works canteens, DIY stores, etc). You are very pleased with this. It has taken a great deal of time and effort to achieve and you have enjoyed the challenge. It is so much more interesting chasing new business than taking routine orders from corner shops.

You have taken to using the phone instead of visiting many of them. There seem to be hundreds of them. Your manager told you last time you met that there were more CTN outlets in your territory than in almost any other territory in the country. Using the phone instead of travelling has allowed you time to invest in wooing your new customers with games of golf. You play a 2 handicap and the chance to combine golf with business is wonderful because next week you are determined to win the Regional Open Championship and the practice has been very useful. The unfortunate result of this is that the level of orders from your CTNs has tailed off. You really ought to get round them again before your area manager starts checking up on you. She has spent some time with you and seems to have found nothing wrong with the way you work but you are aware that she is not happy about the overall sales. You believe that you can turn it around over the Christmas period. You have only got to get around these boring little shops for the orders to come rushing in.

To conceal what you have been doing for the last 9 months, you have had to fabricate the daily and weekly reports and your expenses claims. Your area manager has asked to see you today. As you drive to her office you wonder what she wants to talk about. You suppose it is probably your CTN figures again, but you can deal with them once this championship is over. Not that she needs to know about that – not until you have won it, anyway!

Chapter 7:

Grievance role plays

Like all the other occasions on which managers find themselves face to face with members of their staff, the handling of grievances requires considerable skill in communication. One is likely to be exploring areas of deep concern in which people's feelings are much involved.

Grievances can, of course, arise from many acts or omissions. Problems arise for the manager who may be torn between concern for the individual and the need to support subordinate managers or supervisors in their position and decisions. Equally, the grievance may be over one of the manager's own decisions or actions; in these circumstances the manager may feel uncomfortable with the criticism and feel defensive. This does not encourage the easy solution of the problems raised.

Managers need to demonstrate the wisdom of Solomon in resolving grievances and to have a high degree of tact and sensitivity to go with it.

The skills required for the effective resolution of grievances include:

- questioning;
- listening;
- summarizing and mirroring;
- dealing with emotion and aggression;
- observation, interpretation and judgement;

- influencing skills;
- concentrating on facts, not opinions;
- encouraging self analysis.

Practice in the skills necessary to deal effectively with grievances is very useful and this can quite readily be achieved through the medium of role playing. The following scenarios should allow for these skills and other points to emerge.

THE MISSED PROMOTION
Role Play 26

Time guide Up to 1¼ hours, including time for preparation and debrief.

Participants 2 plus observers.

Equipment Desk, chairs and tables. (Trainers may wish to provide a choice of formal or informal seating for participants to choose their own preferred setting.)

Copies of the individual briefs for players of the complainant and his manager. Copies of both for the observers.

Notes for role players (Handout 4, page 48) if required. Observers' checklists (for an example see Handout 3, page 47).

Flipchart or whiteboard to record points during the debrief.

Video camera, tripod, recorder and TV monitor (if required).

LEARNING POINTS AND SKILLS PRACTISED

- All the general interview skills including questioning, listening, the observation of non-verbal signals and the encouragement of self analysis.
- Gaining an acceptance of the reasons for decisions taken.
- Exploring attitudes and perceptions.
- Suggesting alternative goals to remotivate, and the definition and agreement of plans, targets and training needs.
- Dealing with emotion and feelings of resentment.

Procedure See notes on conducting a role play (Checklist, page 49). Issue briefs to the participants and allow up to 20 minutes for preparation. Meanwhile brief the observers and set up the room to represent the manager's office. Allow play to continue for up to half an hour and then give participants a little time to come out of role before starting the review.

Review See notes on feedback and review in Chapter 2 (Handouts 1 & 2, pages 45 and 46)

In particular, the group should try to answer the following questions.

- How effective was the questioning and listening?
- How well were the employee's feelings explored, emotions dealt with and criticism of the boss accepted?
- How satisfied was the employee with the outcome? Would he still have a sense of grievance?
- Did the employee accept the reasons for not being promoted?
- In the light of the discussions, how could the interview have been handled differently?

HANDOUT
Grievance – the missed promotion

Brief for the manager

Three months ago you promoted one of your workshop supervisors to be the temporary workshop manager. For encouragement you mentioned that there might be a chance to do the job on a permanent basis some day and you wanted to watch his performance. Yesterday you told the supervisor that a new manager was due to start in 2 weeks and asked for as much help as possible for the new manager. He didn't say much and walked out. Today he has formally asked to see you about a grievance he has about the job. It is probably because of the appointment of the new manager. When you asked him to fill the job temporarily, you explained the temporary nature of the job and that you saw it as a chance for him to prove what he could do for possible future promotion.

Frankly, since then you have not been impressed. The workshop has gone on working OK but the costs per service have risen and the productivity has dropped. There have also been too many breakdowns on the road. You have had at least 2 angry transport managers shouting at you about breakdowns that have occurred within hours of the vehicles coming out of the service bay. He seems to have no clue how to handle the staff. There have been all sorts of rumblings from the fitters about this 'little Hitler'. He had always been a very good supervisor, getting on with the job alongside the fitters and you cannot work out quite why he should have become the tyrant that he is now painted.

At no time has he ever come to you and asked for help and whenever you asked him if he needed anything he was so positive that everything was under control that you have given up asking.

In any event, you have now appointed a new manager and things should settle down. You do want the opportunity to talk to the temporary manager to give him some feedback on the way things have gone while he was in the chair. Your plan was to use him as the manager's number 2 with an overall responsibility for scheduling and quality which would give him a greater range of tasks and responsibilities than before. You now have doubts ... it will be interesting to see what in particular he is upset about.

You feel fairly confident that you have handled things reasonably well. If you had any concern about your own actions, it would be that you did not persevere in trying to help him in the new job but he seemed so unwilling to accept any help. You also felt unable to give him any feedback on his performance because it would not have been taken kindly. You had hoped to talk to him at his appraisal next month.

HANDOUT
Grievance – the missed promotion

Brief for the employee with the grievance

Three months ago you were temporarily promoted to the position of workshop manager responsible for the repair of all the company's vehicles and others for contract maintenance customers. At the time your boss led you to believe that it was only a matter of time before the promotion was formalized and you just had to prove that you could do it. Yesterday your boss called you in to tell you that a new manager was starting in 2 weeks' time and that you should now give the new person all the help and support you could. You were so surprised you didn't say anything at the time but now you have had the time to think about it you cannot understand what has gone wrong and you are determined to have it out with your boss. You feel that you have had a really dirty trick played on you. You have worked extremely hard for the last 3 months and as far as you know you have done what was required. Your boss has had no complaints that you have been told about, and only 3 weeks ago you asked, 'How do you think it is going?' No comment was made either way.

The workshop has worked well. The output has remained high and there have been no complaints from transport managers about vehicle availability. While you are not used to the costing and accounting system, as far as you can tell there is no problem there. You would like to have known more about it, though, but have been unwilling to ask for fear of showing yourself up. You were going to ask for some help once the job was yours.

You have had a few problems with the fitters in the shop. You had been working with them as one of their supervisors until 3 months ago, so you felt that you really needed to assert your authority. You have been very strict over timekeeping, break times and absence and have made sure that time has been deducted where necessary.

You have also been particularly anxious to maintain the quality of the work done and have carried out plenty of snap inspections as vehicles are about to go out after servicing. The fitters have given you quite a hard time and you considered disciplinary action against a couple of the noisiest.

You want to be certain that the boss understands the problems you have had and how well you have overcome them. Why should someone who doesn't know the company, the workshop or the vehicles have the job? You can do it. If your boss doesn't like the way you've been doing it, why the blazes hasn't anything been said? And you want to put over that you feel badly treated. You do not know how you can go on working in the workshop with the fitters after all this.

THE LOSS OF OVERTIME
Role Play 27

Time guide Up to 1 hour, including time for preparation and review.

Participants 2 plus observers.

Equipment Desk, chairs and tables.(Trainers may wish to provide a choice of formal or informal seating for participants to choose their own preferred setting.)

Copies of the general brief for everyone. Copies of the individual briefs for players of the complainant and the manager. Copies of both for the observers.

Notes for role players (Handout 4, page 48) if required. Observers' checklists (for an example see Handout 3, page 47).

Flipchart or whiteboard to record points during the debrief.

Video camera, tripod, recorder and TV monitor (if required).

LEARNING POINTS AND SKILLS PRACTISED

- All the general interview skills including questioning, listening, the observation of non-verbal signals and the encouragement of the exploration of others' points of view.
- The exploration of attitudes and perceptions.
- Dealing with emotion and feelings of resentment.
- Gaining an acceptance of the reasons for decisions taken.

Procedure See notes on conducting role plays (Checklist, page 49). Issue briefs to the participants and allow up to 20 minutes for preparation. Meanwhile brief the observers and set up the room to represent the manager's office. Allow play to continue for up to 20 minutes and then give participants a little time to come out of role before starting the review.

Review See notes on feedback and review in Chapter 2 (Handouts 1 & 2, pages 45 and 46).

In particular, the group should try to answer the following questions as part of the review.

- How good were the communication skills used? (Questioning, listening, summarizing, probing, etc.)
- How well were the employee's feelings explored?
- Was the employee left with a feeling of grievance and how positive did he feel about the future?
- Was the employee convinced of the need for the overtime ban? If not, why not?
- How will this interview affect the employee's attitude to the company and work in future?

HANDOUT
Grievance – the loss of overtime

General brief for all

You work for a large regional public utility company. Every day your computer system prints a large number of bills on continuous stationery. These need to be split, burst and enclosed. The operation is carried out mechanically, but there is a great deal of handling, stacking and sorting of the bills and the other promotional and advisory materials that need to be enclosed with them.

The enclosing itself is done on machines that need to be fed continuously with small bundles of the bills and other materials including window envelopes. These materials must be riffled and flipped to free and separate each item to ensure ease of enclosing on the machine. At the take-off end of the machine the filled envelopes are bundled and sorted for the Post Office. All these operations require a great deal of manual manipulation.

Over the last year there has been a disturbing increase in the number of cases of repetitive strain injuries or complaints (tenosynovitis, bursitis, etc) being suffered by enclosing-machine operators. Whether this is due to the work itself or whether there are other factors (one sufferer is a keen handbell ringer, another knits a lot) is not clear. The company has conducted several surveys including those by the company doctor and by an ergonomist, and has started to monitor the incidence of complaints.

The symptoms are pain in the wrists or lower arms. In one or two cases here, and in others described in medical literature, the condition has gradually deteriorated to the point where the pain is such that the operators cannot continue to work. Longer-term damage and impairment of wrist function has occurred in some of these cases.

© David Turner 1992, published by Kogan Page

Recently the rule has been issued by the company that anyone complaining of pains in the arm will not be permitted to work overtime. It is felt that if the work is the cause of the problem, then prolonging the exposure to it should be avoided.

HANDOUT
Grievance – the loss of overtime

Brief for the manager

You are the manager of the customer accounts department of a large regional utility company. Your customers, both domestic and commercial, are billed quarterly following a cycle of meter inspections and consumption estimates. This leaves you with the need to enclose a large number of bills daily. You have the number of machines necessary for reasonable levels of output and these are manned by full-time staff.

Recent marketing efforts and the resultant larger customer numbers have increased both overall volumes of bills to be enclosed and the number of items to be enclosed in each envelope. So far you have been unable to convince the powers-that-be of the need to increase manning levels or invest in more or faster machines. Your department now has to work overtime 2 or 3 nights a week. This means that the recent ban on overtime for those people who have complained of pains in the arms leaves you occasionally with a backlog when insufficient people are willing to work late. Since the cause of the pains is as yet unclear, you agree with the need to reduce overtime for those affected and support absolutely the need to protect people as far as possible. There is also the problem of possible claims for injury from employees in the future. You must be seen to be doing everything that is reasonable to prevent injuries at work.

One of your staff, who has asked to see you about this ban, has recently been seen by the company doctor and diagnosed as suffering from repetitive strain problems, so has been banned from doing overtime. This particular employee had always been the first in the queue for overtime.

HANDOUT
Grievance – the loss of overtime

Brief for the employee

You work on the enclosing machines and you have done so for the last 6 years. In the last year you have developed occasional pains in your right wrist which you put down to the constant flicking of the material to separate it before loading the machines. You have now started to do it a different way using both hands with the materials on the table. This seems to help and you haven't had the pain much since you started doing this.

Your partner has just been made redundant, so you are now the sole breadwinner. You always liked to work overtime when it was available, it helped to pay for a holiday, and now it is even more important that you earn money from overtime.

You are sure that you have the problem solved, your wrist is getting better and anyway, whose wrist is it? Surely you can decide if you are fit enough to work, so why has the firm forbidden you overtime work just as there seems to be a bit more available?

When the pain started, you made the mistake of telling your supervisor about it. There seemed to be quite a lot of people complaining and it made sense to tell about your symptoms too. You now wish that you had said nothing about it to anyone. You did have a couple of weeks off after you saw the company doctor with it. He insisted that you rest the wrist entirely.

You are about to have it out with the manager. You need some of that overtime and you don't care if it will hurt you a bit: you are sure it won't anyway.

POOR WORKING CONDITIONS

Role Play 28

Time guide Up to 1½ hours, including time for preparation and review.

Participants 3 plus observers.

Equipment Desk, chairs and tables.

Copies of the general brief for all and copies of the individual briefs for players of the union official and the manager. A copy of the union brief for the factory shop steward. Copies of everything for the observers.

Notes for role players (Handout 4, page 48) if required. Observers' checklists (for an example see Handout 3, page 47).

Flipchart or whiteboard to record points during the debrief.

Video camera, tripod, recorder and TV monitor (if required).

LEARNING POINTS AND SKILLS PRACTISED

- All the general interview skills including questioning, listening, the observation of non-verbal signals and the encouragement of the exploration of others' points of view.
- The exploration of attitudes and perceptions and the fundamental causes of the grievance.
- Dealing with emotion and feelings of resentment.
- Gaining an acceptance of the reasons for decisions taken and cooperation in implementing them.
- Establishing trust and providing reassurance.

Procedure See notes on conducting role plays (Checklist, page 49). Issue briefs to the participants and allow up to 20 minutes for preparation. Meanwhile brief the observers and set up the room to represent the manager's office. Allow play to continue for up to 30 minutes and then give participants a little time to come out of role before starting the review.

Review See notes on feedback and review in Chapter 2 (Handouts 1 & 2, pages 45 and 46).

In particular, the group should try to answer the following questions.

- How good were the communication skills used? (Questioning, listening, summarising, probing, etc.)
- How well were the employees' feelings explored?
- Was the official left with a feeling that there was an end to the problems and did he feel positive about the future?
- How will this interview affect the employees' attitude to the company and work in future?
- What could have been done to make the full time union official's involvement unnecessary?
- How receptive to ideas for improvement was the manager?

HANDOUT
Grievance – poor working conditions

General information for all

Carstairs Joinery Ltd is an old established firm employing about 250 people. Over 200 of these are employed in the factory, working on the machinery that produces, among other things, knockdown furniture (sold in flatpacks), mouldings for the building trade and a range of prestige kitchen units under contract for one of the big names.

The factory is a comparatively old building in which the facilities for staff are no better than adequate. The space available for manoeuvre is very limited, the noise is only just below legal limits, the guarding of machinery is safe but ageing and the dust extraction is very poor.

These conditions, coupled with comparatively low wages and (it must be admitted) poor management, have led to poor industrial relations. Things were not improved when an overseas company took over Carstairs, sacked many of the old management, made redundant 22 staff from the shop floor and the offices and appointed a new management team. As a result, the factory staff fought for and obtained formal recognition for their trades union to represent them to the company. They have 100 per cent membership.

As part of the new owner's investment plans, which have been explained in detail to the staff, the factory is being extended. The extension will house new machinery space, an improved dust extraction plant and enhanced facilities (rest rooms, canteen and toilets) for the staff. The work started 2 months ago and was scheduled to last for 3 months. Three weeks ago the building work stopped at the point where the steelwork of the new building was up, the roof on and the wall between old and new had been removed. It is March in a cold spring. The factory is now almost impossible to heat, the draughts make the dust problem worse than usual and access to and from offices, toilets and the car park are now via muddy outdoor paths. Attempts have been made to alleviate the worst of the problems with tarpaulins, space heaters, and giving longer and more frequent breaks to staff with hot drinks available free.

Staff have been told that the original contractors have gone into liquidation and that the company is trying to sort out the mess. The management and the union representatives have met several times to try to sort out the problems. But it is still not good.

Two days ago the staff held a meeting and agreed that they would ask the local area union official to become involved to try to sort it out. He has agreed and is due to see the management today.

HANDOUT
Grievance – poor working conditions

Brief for the factory manager

You are the factory manager of Carstairs. The last 3 weeks have been awful. Ever since the building contractors went bust you have been struggling to keep things going and trying to overcome the worst of the problems the unfinished job has left.

You have arranged for the gap in the wall to be sealed off with tarpaulin, you have hired space heaters, and you have arranged to double the number and increase the length of breaks for your staff. You are providing an almost continuous supply of hot drinks and the vending machines are dispensing free drinks. This wretched cold spell of weather doesn't help.

The worst problems are associated with dust, noise and fumes. The unscheduled opening allows the wind to blow in, distributing not only all the sawdust and shavings liberally everywhere but also fumes and noise from the traffic on the bypass along the rear wall and the fumes from vehicles loading your products at the loading bay. None of these things was a problem until this wall was taken down. The dust extraction system, never very good, is now terrible. The contractors had to remove part of the ducting and reposition some fans, and the new configuration is not really very effective. Several machines now emit large quantities of dust only for it to be blown around in the gusts of wind.

Negotiations are under way with a new contractor to continue the work. So far you have been unable to find anyone able to start work immediately. You are not very hopeful that things are going to get straight very quickly and you have avoided telling staff anything for fear of upsetting them with the fact that there is no end in sight.

They know the building firm went bust and they know what steps you have taken to try and help, but that is all so far.

The local full-time union official rang you yesterday to say that his members were very unhappy about what was happening and that he wished to come and see you. He was muttering darkly about industrial action. You cannot afford a stoppage, particularly on the kitchen units since they are very profitable and the contract ties you to providing a continuous supply.

You are sympathetic, but short of shutting down, and you cannot afford that, you don't know what else you can do.

HANDOUT
Grievance – poor working conditions

Brief for the union official and the shop steward

At a union meeting after hours 2 days ago, the factory staff wished the full-time union official to become involved. A meeting is arranged to take place shortly. The pair of you will attend. Your intention is to make certain that the management are aware of the strength of feeling among the staff about the poor conditions and to get something done about it. You are prepared to threaten industrial action. However, no one is working overtime in these conditions and no one actually wants a strike, so it can only be a threat. You could perhaps threaten to call in the Factory Inspector or the Health and Safety people.

You are sure that if the management could get the materials, staff could put up a really effective wind-proof barrier. They could make duckboarding for the pathways and do some better jury rigging on the extraction system. There might need to be some extra time and effort from the small maintenance team, who are normally flat out keeping machinery and extraction equipment going. You believe that it would be far better to lose most of a few days' production and use volunteers from among the staff to restore some sort of order and improve the conditions for everyone. It might even give a new sense of teamwork to the workforce.

There must be some local self-employed tradesmen who could help as well. It just needs a lead, some imagination and a bit of organization. At the moment the staff are demoralized, uncertain and grumbling. They need to be told what is happening. In fact, you have a sneaking suspicion that if the management had come out in the open and explained the problems there would not have been this fuss now. Perhaps that could happen yet.

You are going to take a hard line. Something must be done. But if the manager you see this afternoon isn't coming up with anything then you can throw in these ideas and hints of action if you don't see some improvement.

THE CHANGE OF OFFICES
Role Play 29

Time guide Up to 1¼ hours, including time for preparation and review.

Participants 2 plus observers.

Equipment Desk, chairs and tables. (Trainers may wish to provide a choice of formal or informal seating for participants to choose their own preferred setting.)

A copy of the general brief for all and copies of the individual briefs for the players and copies of everything for the observers.

Notes for role players (Handout 4, page 48) if required. Observers' checklists (for an example see Handout 3, page 47).

Flipchart or whiteboard to record points during the debrief.

Video camera, tripod, recorder and TV monitor (if required).

LEARNING POINTS AND SKILLS PRACTISED

- All the general interview skills including questioning, listening, the observation of non-verbal signals and the encouragement of the exploration of others' points of view.
- The exploration of attitudes and perceptions and the fundamental causes of the grievance.
- Dealing with emotion and feelings of resentment.
- Gaining an acceptance of the reasons for decisions taken.
- Establishing trust and providing reassurance.

Procedure See notes on conducting role plays (Checklist, page 49). Issue briefs to the participants and allow up to 20 minutes for preparation. Meanwhile brief the observers and set up the room to represent the director's office. Allow play to continue for up to 30 minutes and then give participants a little time to come out of role before starting the review.

Review See notes on feedback and review in Chapter 2 (Handouts 1 & 2, pages 45 and 46).

In particular, the group should try to answer the following questions.

- How good were the communication skills used? (Questioning, listening, summarizing, probing, etc.)
- How well were the employee's feelings explored?
- Was the employee left with a feeling that there was an end to the problems and did he feel positive about the future?
- Was the employee satisfied with the outcome? If not, why not?
- How will this interview affect the employee's attitude to the company and work in future?
- What was the director's general attitude? Was it appropriate?

HANDOUT
Grievance – the change of offices

General brief for all

Your company works primarily in property development and construction.

Two months ago the company was taken over by another organization and is now one of its divisions. The board is retained as a subsidiary board, but a new chief executive has been put in place by the parent company. He is making a large number of changes with a view to improving profits and changing the image of your organization and is keen to see them implemented. All the directors, conscious of their vulnerability to being replaced at short notice, are making strenuous efforts to see that the new man's wishes are fulfilled.

Marketing has, hitherto, taken a low-key approach and has been led by the administration director, Monica. Her major concern has been to sell or let the properties once developed and she and the sales manager, Eric, have acted together to achieve that. Results have been very good. Very little completed property, either commercial or domestic, has remained empty for long and there is little empty property on the books at present. The company employs a national chain of estate agents to do most of the detailed work. Eric has been responsible for liaising with them, producing sales literature and running the small customer service section that deals with any concerns the new owners and tenants raise.

As administration director, Monica is also responsible for the whole of the headquarters building and its staff.

HANDOUT
Grievance – the change of offices

Brief for the director

You are Monica, the administration director of the company. Apart from the marketing side, your principal area of responsibility is the headquarters offices with a staff of some 150 people.

One of the changes demanded by the new chief executive has been the appointment of a marketing executive as 'marketing consultant'. This post, which reports to you, is a senior one and the new job holder was effectively appointed by the chief executive. You are happy with both the new post and the person chosen and you were involved in the appointment. The speed with which it was done, however, causes you some concern. The new man is to raise the profile of the company, get its name recognized and have it associated with quality and a care for the environment.

Your office accommodation is limited. When the new appointment was made Eric, the sales manager, was away on holiday for 3 weeks. He had arranged several months ago to take an extended holiday this year, for his silver wedding and to visit his son in Australia. Because of the speed of the appointment, Eric was unaware that it was happening and you have had to give his old office to the new person who started today. Today is also Eric's first day back after his holiday. He should have returned last week but his plane was grounded in Indonesia on the way home and he lost 3 days. He has just rung you in a very agitated state and wishes to see you.

The reasons that forced you to make this decision, which you knew would hurt, were threefold. First, the new person, with the influence of the chief executive behind him, needed an office in keeping with his seniority. Second, there was no other office available, although there was a small office at the back which had always been used for storage. This is not a particularly good office and will need refurbishment. You have already allocated funds for this. This little office you have allocated to Eric, and his desk, etc, have been moved in there. Third, Eric's secretary will now be shared between him and the new marketing consultant, and as there is nowhere else for the secretary's furniture to move to she is staying where she is, a long way from Eric.

Moving Eric was the obvious solution to your problem. The job he has been doing remains to be done; it may even be enhanced as the profile of the marketing function grows. The only problem is a perceived knock to his status and you must try to get him back on your side.

HANDOUT
Grievance – the change of offices

Brief for the sales manager

You are Eric, the sales manager for the company. You have always felt that you do a good job and your director has never led you to believe otherwise. In fact you thought you got on very well with her.

This morning you return to work after a somewhat prolonged holiday, to find that your office has been moved, that you are now to share your secretary and a new 'marketing consultant' has been appointed.

Your holiday was for you and your wife to visit Australia to see your son and his family. You celebrated your silver wedding with them. You had arranged the 3 weeks for this holiday months in advance as it was a special occasion. It was a great time and it was only marred by the 3 days' enforced delay in Indonesia on the way home; the plane had a fault and apparently no other one was available. Otherwise you would have been back in the middle of last week. So you have now been away for nearly 4 weeks.

Before you left you had no idea that a new marketing post was to be made. Your 'new' office is tiny, dirty and a long way from where your secretary still sits outside your old office. Why have you got to have such a poky, dingy little cupboard? Surely things don't have to move so fast that you are pensioned off to some crummy hole like this? Is somebody trying to tell you something...? What is so special about this new person that you have to move out without so much as a by your leave? You are going to give your boss Monica, the administration director, a piece of your mind. And why have you to share your secretary anyway? She was always complaining of being too busy when she worked for you alone. You always got on well with her though. It doesn't seem any fairer to her than it does to you. Still, she hasn't had to move offices!

When you got in this morning you rang the director as soon as you discovered what was going on. You are on your way to see her now.

PERSECUTION?

Role Play 30

Time guide Up to 2 hours, including time for preparation and debrief.

Participants 3 plus observers.

Equipment Desk, chairs and tables. (Trainers may wish to provide a choice of formal or informal seating for participants to choose their own preferred setting.)

Copies of the individual briefs for players of the complainant, his manager and the supervisor. Copies of all three for the observers.

Notes for role players (Handout 4, page 48) if required. Observers' checklists (for an example see Handout 3, page 47).

Flipchart or whiteboard to record points during the debrief.

Video camera, tripod, recorder and TV monitor (if required).

LEARNING POINTS AND SKILLS PRACTISED

- All the general interview skills including questioning, listening, the observation of non-verbal signals and the encouragement of self analysis.
- Gaining an acceptance of the reasons for decisions taken.
- Exploring attitudes and perceptions.
- Suggesting alternative goals to remotivate, the definition and agreement of plans, targets and training needs.
- Dealing with emotion and feelings of resentment.

Procedure See notes on conducting a role play (Checklist, page 49). In this 2-part role play the manager should interview both the employee and the supervisor. Issue briefs to the participants and allow up to 20 minutes for preparation. Meanwhile brief the observers and set up the room to represent the manager's office. Allow play to continue for up to 40 minutes (for both interviews). The manager should be permitted to decide whom to see first and whether the player currently not involved should remain in the room. Then give participants a little time to come out of role before starting the review.

Review See notes on feedback and review in Chapter 2 (Handouts 1 & 2, pages 45 and 46).

In particular, the group should try to answer the following questions.

- How effective was the questioning and listening?
- How well were the employee's feelings explored, emotions dealt with and criticism of the supervisor handled?
- How satisfied was the employee with the outcome? Would he still have a sense of grievance?
- How would the supervisor feel about the final outcome of the interviews?

HANDOUT
Grievance – persecution?

Brief for the manager

You are the production manager in an engineering company which employs some 50 people and produces parts for the aircraft industry. The work is done on a variety of machines and the shop floor is organized so that there are 3 teams, each with its own supervisor. Each team is responsible for monitoring its own quality and earns a bonus, paid weekly, based on the output from the team in the week.

One of your employees, aged 18, has formally asked to see you as he is aggrieved about the way he is treated by his supervisor.

You have spoken to the supervisor who tells you that this particular lad is a waster. He makes no effort and his performance affects the earnings, in bonus terms, of the rest of the team. The level of rejects from his work is the highest in the team and there is the highest number of breakdowns on the machines that he minds. The supervisor tells you that he has been on at the lad for ages and was on the point of taking some form of disciplinary action against him. Had this complaint not arisen, your supervisor was going to talk to you about discipline today. The other thing that your supervisor tells you is that the lad is surly, disrespectful and forever answering back and coming out with almost abusive language when told off for poor quality or a breakdown. When asked, the supervisor admitted that the employee's timekeeping and attendance record was excellent.

Your own impression of the employee is of a cheerful, sociable and apparently industrious young man. The supervisor has had problems with young employees before. He appears to want to treat them like apprentices of many years ago. He seems to have no rapport with younger people and has a very directive, prescriptive way of dealing with them. You have had words with the supervisor before about some instances you have noticed in the past. There have been no problems, that you are aware of, for some months. This is the first time anyone has actually formally notified you that they wish to discuss a grievance with you that concerns this supervisor's behaviour to them.

You mentioned this concern to your supervisor but he denied any overbearing behaviour and was quite abrupt and walked off, saying you had spoken to him about that already. You have arranged to hear the employee's complaint in a few minutes.

HANDOUT
Grievance – persecution?

Brief for the employee

You are 18 years old and you have been working in this engineering factory for 6 months. The job is machine minding and you are responsible for 3 milling and grinding machines. The workshop produces parts for the aircraft industry.

You are a member of one of 3 teams in the workshop, each one working under its own supervisor. Each team is responsible for monitoring its own quality and earns a weekly bonus on its output. Your team almost always has the lowest reject rate and the highest bonus each week. You enjoy the work and you have some good friends among the rest of the workshop. Your one big problem is your supervisor; he has really got it in for you. You have learnt the job very quickly since you came here but no credit for that goes to the supervisor. After your first day he left you to pick up what you could from the rest of the team. Because everyone is going for the quality and bonus they have told you what you asked but not much more. The result is that for all but the last few weeks your productivity has been low, you have had quite a few rejects and one of your machines keeps breaking down. Every time you get a reject, every day when your totals are low, and every time a machine stops, this supervisor is down on you like a ton of bricks.

You started by trying to explain that there were still things you did not understand, asking him to help you, but he did not listen. It is obviously pointless trying to get help from him and since all he ever does is shout at you, you have taken to ignoring him. You have let him know, subtly, what you think of him. He keeps going on about the old days and how good it would have been for you to have been through the same hard school. When you said that you would be happy to go through it if only some fool would tell you how everything was supposed to work, he got very upset and shouted that he would never have dared to talk to his foreman like that when he was your age. The man has no idea about getting people to work for him. The rest of the team put up with him and they have been with him a long time. He does plan the work well, ensures the minimum of delays and so the team does do well on the whole for quality and bonus.

The machine that keeps breaking down, you discover, is the oldest in the place and has been behaving in that way for the last 5 years at least. Yesterday it broke down again; this time it probably was your fault but it is the first time you have really had to admit that. He went crazy, shouting and waving his fist. He accused you of sabotage and threatened to take disciplinary action to get you fired. You shouted back, called him a few names and told your manager at break time that you wished to see him to make a complaint about your supervisor's behaviour to you.

HANDOUT
Grievance – persecution?

Brief for the supervisor

You are one of 3 team supervisors in an engineering company which employs some 50 people and produces parts for the aircraft industry. The work is done on a variety of machines and the shop floor is organized so that there are 3 teams, each with its own supervisor. Each team is responsible for monitoring its own quality and earns a bonus, paid weekly, based on the output from the team in the week. Your team generally obtains the highest weekly bonus and the lowest reject rate.

You have been with the company for 24 years and have worked your way up from apprentice. One of your team, a young 18-year-old, is causing you some problems. He seems to have no idea about the work. He is forever making mistakes on quality; his reject rate is the highest in the team. His output is also the lowest in the team, although this has improved just recently. Another problem you have with him is his inability to look after the machines. He is always having breakdowns and his down time is the highest in the works.

A young lad like this should really be working hard, listening to his elders and betters and be prepared to do as he is told; just as you did when you were an apprentice. There's no use giving a boy a man's job unless he can do it right and this lad just does not seem to have what it takes. You have tried very hard to get him to accept what is required but he just doesn't seem to want to know. You let him know every time that he fails to produce enough and when his reject rates are too high. On top of it all the boy is insolent. He raises his eyes to heaven when you tell him about his rejects and he turns away while you are talking to him. He seems to make no effort to hide the fact that he doesn't like or respect you. He was always badgering you with stupid questions about little things he ought to have known but that seems to have stopped now.

Yesterday you really had to tear into him when he called you a fool when you were talking to him about another breakdown. You let him know that your patience was wearing thin and that you were considering some form of disciplinary action against him for his failure to perform up to the required standard.

When you heard that he had made a complaint to the manager you were furious and went straight in to tell the manager the real situation. He then had the nerve to suggest that you might be being too harsh on the lad – something he had a go at you about (over another series of events) a few months ago. Of course you are not being too harsh; you heard what the manager had to say last time and you have taken it to heart. No, this lad just isn't what you want around the place. He can't take it.

PAYING FOR QUALIFICATIONS

Role Play 31

Time guide Up to 1 hour, including 20 minutes for preparation and 20 minutes for debrief.

Participants 2 plus observers.

Equipment Desk, chairs and tables. (Trainers may wish to provide a choice of formal or informal seating for participants to choose their own preferred setting.)

Copies of the individual briefs for players of the manager and assistant. Copies of both for the observers.

Notes for role players (Handout 4, page 48) if required. Observers' checklists (for an example see Handout 3, page 47).

Flipchart or whiteboard to record points during the debrief.

Video camera, tripod, recorder and TV monitor (if required).

LEARNING POINTS AND SKILLS PRACTISED

- All the general interview skills including questioning, listening and the observation of non-verbal signals.
- The exploration of attitudes, clarification and understanding of aspirations.
- Planning initial approaches with the other person's motivation in mind.
- Selling benefits and advantages in order to overcome objections.
- Finding means other than cash to motivate staff.

Procedure See notes on the conduct of role plays (Checklist, page 49). Issue briefs to the participants and allow up to 20 minutes for preparation. Meanwhile brief the observers and set up the room to represent the manager's office. Allow play to continue for up to 20 minutes. Then give participants a little time to come out of role before starting the review.

Review See notes on feedback and review in chapter 2 (Handouts 1 & 2, pages 45 and 46).

In particular, the group should try to answer the following questions as part of the review.

- How sensitively did the manager handle the situation?
- Did the employee feel that the problem was understood?
- Was she happy with the outcome?
- Was there an acceptable way forward?
- Did the manager take account of the employee's aspirations and wishes?
- Were there any other actions the manager could have taken to help to resolve this problem?

HANDOUT
Grievance – paying for qualifications

Brief for the library manager

You are the manager, or librarian in charge, of a specialist library in an institution. You have been in charge for the last 7 years. When you started you worked alone but the volume of work, especially researching, has increased so much that you now have 3 staff working for you.

The longest serving of these you recruited 5 years ago. This particular person has been a great help to you and seems to have a natural flair for the job and a real enthusiasm for it. You rely heavily on her skill, enthusiasm and effort and she naturally deputizes for you in your absence. Her work and her attitude to it are much appreciated by you and by the many highly qualified users of the library. She has no formal qualifications in librarianship or any degree. She has just the normal results obtained from a school career to age 18 and she is now 28. She is paid at the highest clerical grade, Grade 5.

The second of your staff is a part-time clerical assistant who has no librarianship duties and is a Grade 2. The third member of staff you recruited 18 months ago after a directive from the centre decreed that staff appointed to this sort of job should in future have either professional qualifications or a degree. This chap is a very personable and cheerful person who appeared at interview to be willing, outgoing and able. He has a degree in English but no librarianship qualification.

Unfortunately, he is not a success. His understanding of the needs of the job is poor and there is no apparent enthusiasm for it. The quality of the information he produces in researching is poor and there have been a few remarks passed about it. There is little commitment to the job; he is very unwilling to put in extra hours - something that the rest of you do as a matter of course when it is necessary. There is not much you can actually take him to task for, but he does no more than he has to. Because of his degree, he is paid at a grade two levels higher than your first assistant and is a Grade 7. The difference in cash terms is quite significant.

The grading system is not flexible. The highest clerical grade, Grade 5, is as high as one can progress without formal qualification or supervisory responsibilities. Grade 6 is the first level of supervision and Grade 7 is the entry level for graduates and those with relevant professional qualifications as well as for more senior supervisors. You are on Grade 8, the first management grade. The institute is very academically orientated but is not noted for its commitment to the development of its more junior staff. The staff member who is a Grade 5 and has been with you for 5 years has been unhappy about the pay differential for some time and has now asked to see you, formally, about it.

HANDOUT
Grievance – paying for qualifications

Brief for the library assistant

You work in a specialist library in an institution. You have been working there for 5 years and were the first assistant that your manager, the librarian in charge, recruited.

You are paid as a Grade 5, which is the highest clerical grade in the organization. You left school at 18 and had the usual exams from your school career. You have no other qualifications. For five years you worked as a clerk in an insurance office before getting this job. You love it here; you enjoy the work and are fascinated with the material that you look after and research through. Even the basic chores of running a library you find satisfying. You feel that you do a good job – your manager has said so several times and some of the library users have been very complimentary when you have researched and presented information for them.

There are two other members of staff; one is a part-time clerk/typist and the other is doing the same job as yourself as a library assistant. This one is a bit of a nuisance. He is not very interested, has little enthusiasm and doesn't do a high quality job unless pushed. He will do all he has to but no more. You are always having to clear up or finish off after him and he frequently passes work over to you saying that he doesn't know how to do it. You have noticed that some of the library users have started to avoid asking him questions or for assistance. Fair enough, if he is not a particularly good worker he is at least cheerful and quite pleasant to work with. What really annoys you is that, despite the extra work and effort that you put in (to good effect, apparently) he is on a grade two steps higher than you, at Grade 7.

Apparently, the reason for this is that just before he started, the centre decreed that new starters for this type of job should be professionally qualified or have a degree. This chap has a degree. The rules of the grading system are not flexible. The highest clerical grade, Grade 5 (which you are) is as high as one can progress without formal qualification or supervisory responsibilities. Grade 6 is the first level of supervision and Grade 7 is the entry level for graduates and those with relevant professional qualifications as well as for more senior supervisors.

You have been upset about this ever since the graduate started 18 months ago. Since yesterday, when he left you with yet another batch of work to be finished after he had gone home, you have decided to speak to the librarian in charge about it. You have mentioned your dissatisfaction before but only in passing.

Chapter 8:

Managing people at work

The management of people at work is the fundamental task in which managers are involved all the time. In practice, the techniques used are the same as those employed in appraisal, discipline, grievance and even negotiation. In some ways you could say that these activities are themselves techniques for use in the management of people at work.

The activities that recur regularly are such things as delegation, counselling, praising, giving feedback, giving instruction, consulting, persuading, influencing, managing poor performance and so on. Each of these is, in itself, an exercise in inter-personal communication skills via the medium of a face-to-face interview between the manager and the individual. The skills associated with interviewing are, therefore, appropriate and include:

- assertiveness;
- gaining agreement and commitment;
- the use of questions;
- listening effectively;
- understanding body language;
- dealing with emotion;
- giving positive and negative feedback;
- establishing facts;
- controlling conversations;
- encouraging self analysis.

The following scenarios provide the opportunity for these skills to be practised and appreciated.

THE UNDER-ACHIEVER

Role Play 32

Time guide Up to 1½ hours, including 30 minutes for preparation and 30 minutes for debrief.

Participants 2 plus observers.

Equipment Desk, chairs and tables. (Trainers may wish to provide a choice of formal or informal seating for participants to choose their own preferred setting.)

Copies of the individual briefs for players of the employee and the manager. Copies of both for the observers.

Notes for role players (Handout 4, page 48) if required. Observers' checklists (for an example see Handout 3, page 47).

Flipchart or whiteboard to record points raised during the debrief.

Video camera, tripod, recorder and TV monitor (if required).

LEARNING POINTS AND SKILLS PRACTISED

- All the general interview skills including questioning, listening, the giving of both positive and negative feedback and the observation of non-verbal signals.
- Gaining agreement and commitment for the necessary changes to take place.
- The exploration of attitudes and perceptions.
- Dealing with emotion and the resentment of criticism.
- The firm definition and agreement of plans, targets and standards.

Procedure See notes on the conduct of role plays (Checklist, page 49). Issue handouts to participants and brief them. Allow up to ½ hour for preparation. Meanwhile brief the observers and set the room up to represent the manager's office. Allow play to continue for up to 30 minutes and then give a few moments for players to come out of role before starting the review.

Review See notes on feedback and review in Chapter 2 (Handouts 1 & 2, pages 45 and 46).

In particular, the group should try to answer the following questions as part of the review.

- Did the manager achieve her aim?
- How well did the manager encourage self analysis?
- Was the need for change accepted and standards agreed?
- How well did the manager involve the employee in agreeing the plan for the required standards to be met?
- Who did most of the talking? Did the manager listen well?

HANDOUT
The under-achiever

Brief for the manager

You are the manager of a small office in a large market research, advertising and marketing company, employing 6 young graduates. Your staff work on a variety of tasks involving the statistical analysis of surveys, the extrapolation of results and some interpretation of trends. All this is done with the aid of some sophisticated computer equipment.

Your staff tend not to stay with you for long. The normal pattern is that they master the analysis and interpretation of data then they move on to other activities in the company. Your office is the 'reception area' for new graduates as the grounding it provides in the facts behind the marketing and advertising 'hype' is considered invaluable. Part of your role is to advise the company about the calibre of your young people, their suitability for other departments and when a transfer would be appropriate.

One graduate trainee that you have is not performing as well as you would like. She has a first class honours degree in Regional Science and has always expressed an interest in the analysis of regional differences in purchasing patterns, in the effectiveness of differing marketing approaches in different areas and in devising new strategies to meet the differing demands. You were very impressed with her when she first arrived 6 months ago and foresaw that she would be ready to move on to new things quite quickly. However, her performance over the last few weeks has been very erratic. This is particularly disappointing to you as she ought to be capable of making an excellent job of it.

She has started to come in late occasionally, and is always away on the dot. More significantly her accuracy is declining and several quite major errors of calculation have been traced to her. In one survey some information had been ignored or missed and some figures accounted for twice: the net result was highly misleading. Fortunately you had double checked some of her work as part of the routine, and found the error before it became too costly. In another instance a regional TV advertisement campaign, planned on the basis of her research, had to be cancelled after the trends were found to be incorrectly calculated.

She appears to have lost concentration and to be losing interest in the work. She is becoming uncooperative and appears to resent criticism. It is time to approach her about the problem and explain what you need from her in terms of accuracy and quality.

You have asked to see her in a few minutes.

HANDOUT
The under-achiever

Brief for the graduate

You were employed by this company about 6 months ago as a graduate entrant. It is normal in this market research, advertising and marketing company for new graduate entrants to be employed for the first few months in the market research statistical department. This is where you are currently working.

Your first class degree in Regional Science has given you a great interest and enthusiasm for the exploration of regional differences. You are currently concerned with the data emerging from market surveys, analysed and interpreted by you with the aid of computers. This is real child's play to you and after a couple of months you became very bored with it.

At the same time, your father died, leaving you a great deal of money. Earning a living is no longer a real necessity. For the last 4 or 5 years you have done nothing but work hard for exams and now at last you have the chance and the opportunity to live a little. You have acquired a new flat and are busy furnishing it. You have a new boyfriend with whom you have a great deal of fun, going to parties, theatres and places of interest. It is not a particularly serious relationship but it is exciting and you want to make as much of this new-found freedom as you can.

The job, which was becoming boring anyway, has become a way of filling in the time between doing the things you want to do. You know that you have made a few mistakes lately. Recently you missed some data and considered other data twice. On another occasion it was only luck that prevented a TV ad from being made on the basis of the wrong assumptions you drew from a regional survey. But, being honest with yourself, you don't really care. Life is fun and unless they can find you something more interesting to do you might give up and go elsewhere.

Your manager has asked to see you in a few minutes.

BREAKING THE BAD NEWS

Role Play 33

Time guide Up to $1\frac{1}{4}$ hours, including 25 minutes for preparation and 20 minutes for debrief.

Participants 2 plus observers.

Equipment Desk, chairs and tables. (Trainers may wish to provide a choice of formal or informal seating for participants to choose their own preferred setting.)

Copies of the individual briefs for players of the director and the manager. Copies of both for the observers.

Notes for role players (Handout 4, page 48) if required. Observers' checklists (for an example see Handout 3, page 47).

Flipchart or whiteboard to record points raised during the debrief.

Video camera, tripod, recorder and TV monitor (if required).

LEARNING POINTS AND SKILLS PRACTISED

- All the general interview skills including questioning, listening, the giving of both positive and negative feedback and the observation of non-verbal signals.
- Sensitivity in conveying bad news.
- The exploration of attitudes and perceptions in attempting to retain motivation.
- Dealing with emotion and resentment.

Procedure See notes on conducting role plays (Checklist, page 49). Issue handouts to participants and brief them. Allow up to 25 minutes for preparation. Meanwhile brief the observers and set the room up to represent the manager's office. Allow play to continue for up to 30 minutes and then give a few moments for players to come out of role before starting the review.

Review See notes on feedback and review in Chapter 2 (Handouts 1 & 2, pages 45 and 46).

In particular, the group should try to answer the following questions as part of the review.

- How sensitively did the director handle the situation?
- Did the manager understand and accept the reasons for not being promoted?
- How well did the director encourage self analysis?
- Did the director leave the manager with a proper sense of his own worth? How will he approach the job from now on?
- Who did most of the talking? Did the director listen well?

HANDOUT
Breaking the bad news

Brief for the retiring production director

You are about to retire as the production director of this publishing company. At yesterday's board meeting the final choice was made for your successor. After a selection process in which 2 outsiders were considered alongside your current production manager, it was agreed that one of the outside candidates should be appointed.

Your current manager was aware that others were being considered and you had discussed with him the possibility of his becoming a director. In fact you had considered him right for the appointment until this final board meeting. You have had a few reservations about his maturity, his ability to handle stress and about his tact and diplomacy but technically he is very good. You felt that he would grow to meet the responsibility. Comparing him with the other candidates at the final board meeting you came to recognize that his reactions under stress, his lack of tact and his tendency to take personally any criticism of his staff or his department would make him an uncomfortable member of the board.

Examples of his recent behaviour illustrate the problem. Recently a whole batch of paper he had ordered turned out to be the wrong size. Production at the printer's was stopped for 3 days while they waited for new supplies. For weeks afterwards when anyone mentioned the affair he would snap back, disclaiming any responsibility, and walk off in a huff. At a time when production was flat out for the Christmas deliveries, he was working extremely long hours. He wrote off his company car while rushing from one meeting to another, and he dismissed an assistant for a trivial offence during this period, which led to a claim for wrongful dismissal. Two weeks later he was off sick for 3 weeks, having collapsed at a particularly tense committee meeting. The company doctor put the incidents down to an inability to handle stress. Needless to say, hitherto he has failed to accept that he has a problem with stress. On several occasions you and he have had blazing rows about what needed to be done. This was not a problem for you since you know and understand the man. You are also aware that he has had some domestic problems, although you do not know the details.

Before the announcement of the appointment of your successor is made tomorrow you must tell him of the decision and try to get him to accept it. He is still very much needed in the production department. This is a difficult job for you. You feel that he may think you have let him down. However, the new man is a very experienced production specialist, about 8 years younger than your current manager, with an excellent track record in your industry.

HANDOUT
Breaking the bad news

Brief for the production manager

You are the production manager for a publishing company and you have been doing the job for several years. You have been working extremely hard just lately since production volumes are at an all-time high.

For some time now it has been apparent that your boss, the production director, is about to retire. You and she have discussed the situation at length and you are fairly sure that she intends to put your name up for the board position. She hasn't made any promises, but a few remarks she has made suggest that she has got you in mind for the job. It is something you would very much like to do. You have been with this company for a long time and it would be a fitting reward for the efforts you have put in and you would like to see some of your ideas put into practice.

You have been giving it a lot of thought recently and you have concluded that you could do the job. You have considered how you might react to the rest of the board and how you would cope with the added responsibility. You would find it hard at first and you might have to assert yourself a bit to establish your position. You have been criticised in the past for being too quick to lose your temper, and you would have to watch that. During the last few months you have had a few rows with your boss. They haven't been much but you did get a bit excited and you have had to apologize to her a couple of times. So you are aware that, perhaps, you would need to watch your tongue a little.

After all the pressure recently, your boss spoke to you asking how you coped with stress. You were quite happy to say that it was not a problem. Look how the recent workload has been dealt with. Sure, you get a bit het up sometimes, but doesn't everyone under pressure? But you are fine in yourself. Your marriage is a problem, all is not well and one of your children is going off the rails a bit but, thinking about it, you really have coped well with it all. There was that assistant you sacked who claimed wrongful dismissal – and got away with it – that hurt. The company paid up. There was your car smash, you were lucky to get out of that alive. There has been a huge amount of work to be done. You had 3 weeks off after you fainted at work one day. The doctors wouldn't let you back any sooner but you still managed to get the Christmas books delivered on time. The company doctor, too, was asking you questions about stress but you have coped with it rather well.

Your work runs very smoothly on the whole, within budget. The staff are generally content and there has been no bother lately. They are a good bunch and you like to be loyal to them, since you expect loyalty from them. A recent failure by a supplier to provide the right quality of materials was blamed on your staff when production stopped. You let people know what you thought of that and refused to discuss it. It was a supplier error.

Your boss has just rung to see if you are free and will be down to see you in a few minutes – you wonder if she knows about the board appointment yet.

DELEGATING A PROJECT
Role Play 34

Time guide Up to 1½ hours, including 30 minutes for preparation and 20 minutes for debrief.

Participants 2 plus observers.

Equipment Desk, chairs and tables. (Trainers may wish to provide a choice of formal or informal seating for participants to choose their own preferred setting.)

Copies of the individual briefs for players of the manager and the trainee accountant. Copies of both briefs for the observers.

Notes for role players (Handout 4, page 48) if required. Observers' checklists (for an example see Handout 3, page 47).

Flipchart or whiteboard to record points during the debrief.

Video camera, tripod, recorder and TV monitor (if required).

LEARNING POINTS AND SKILLS PRACTISED

- All the general interview skills including questioning, listening and the observation of non-verbal signals.
- Making initial approaches about delegation.
- The exploration of attitudes and gaining commitment to the delegated task.
- Arranging plans for instruction, training or assistance so the delegated task is successfully completed.

Procedure See notes on conducting role plays (Checklist, page 49). Issue handouts to participants and brief them. Allow up to 25 minutes for preparation. Meanwhile brief the observers and set the room up to represent the manager's office. Allow play to continue for up to 30 minutes and then give a few moments for players to come out of role before starting the review.

Review See notes on feedback and review in Chapter 2 (Handouts 1 & 2, pages 45 and 46).

In particular, the group should try to answer the following questions as part of the review.

- How sensitively did the manager handle the situation?
- Did the employee understand and accept the reasons for being asked to do the task? Did she understand the benefits?
- How well did the manager explain what was required?
- Was this the start of an effective delegation?
- Who did most of the talking? Did the manager listen well?

HANDOUT
Delegating a project

Brief for the management accountant

You are the management accountant of a service company. You are responsible for the budgeting process within the company, for the routine monthly reporting against budget and for costing. All these tasks, with the exception of the monthly reporting of actual figures against budget, are carried out manually.

You have a staff of 6, 2 of whom are studying for accountancy exams. One of these budding accountants is very capable but she is becoming bored with the routine duties that she has to perform in your section. She is happiest when working on the materials supplied by the college as part of her studies for an accountancy qualification. Her progress to date in these studies has been extremely quick.

She is a young woman with lots of potential and you do not want to see her lose heart or interest and maybe leave. You have therefore decided to give her a project to complete. Not only can it be submitted, in report form, as part of her assessment for the next grade in her accountancy but it will also be extremely valuable to the department and a project you have wanted completing for some time. It could result in the reduction of the clerical headcount. This project is something in which you feel she could become really involved and so reduce the frustration and boredom she is currently experiencing.

The task is this: you want her to devise a computer system that will speed up the time it takes to provide costing information to the sales force. In essence, it will involve the setting up of a database of unit costs for all the labour, materials and fixed cost aspects of every operation within the company. To achieve it she will have to talk to all the senior managers in the organization, recruit the help of the management services programers and do a significant amount of research into historical accounting information. You want your section to be able to access this database and retrieve a cost, worked out by breaking the job down into its component parts and costing each aspect of it against the database. You hope that the increased accuracy of forecasting will improve the profitability of contracts tendered for and reduce the clerical load in producing the tenders themselves. You would like to see it finished in time for the autumn, in 6 months' time.

There are several benefits to the young woman herself. Firstly, this project will raise her profile in the organization; she will become known about the place. Secondly, as you have already established, it can contribute to her assessments for the exams, and thirdly it will give her the opportunity to become familiar with many aspects of computer systems.

You have arranged to see her to discuss this project.

HANDOUT
Delegating a project

Brief for the trainee accountant

You have been working in the management accounting section of this service company for 2 years now. They are sponsoring you to acquire an accountancy qualification. So far your studies have gone very well and you are really interested in them. The same cannot be said of your work. The section deals with the collection, correlation and publication of the annual budget for the company, reports monthly on each of the budget centres' performance against budget, and provides costings and costing information for the whole organization and the sales force in particular. All of this, with the exception of the monthly reporting of actual figures against budget, are carried out manually.

You find the work tedious, boring and very repetitive. Thank goodness you have the accountancy exam to study for to keep you interested.

Your boss has asked to see you. You do not really know why, but perhaps she wants to take you to task over your lack of enthusiasm. If so you would like to know what you have actually done wrong – so far as you know there have been no major errors. It would be good to have a talk with her, anyway, to bring up the fact that you are very bored with the routine work. Couldn't she find you something more interesting to do? If not you will concentrate on your studies and sit tight for the next 2 years, or until you have your exam behind you. After that, well . . . !

There are two areas of your work that worry you, if only slightly. You are not good with computers – they seem to know you don't like them and misbehave specially. The other problem is shyness. You are not good with people you don't know. It is a good job that much accountancy requires little contact with other people.

Your appointment with the boss is in a few minutes.

SELLING IDEAS TO THE BOSS

Role Play 35

Time guide Up to $1\frac{1}{4}$ hours, including 25 minutes for preparation and 20 minutes for debrief.

Participants 2 plus observers.

Equipment Desk, chairs and tables. (Trainers may wish to provide a choice of formal or informal seating for participants to choose their own preferred setting.)

Copies of the individual briefs for players of the middle and senior managers. Copies of both for the observers.

Notes for role players (Handout 4, page 48) if required. Observers' checklists (for an example see Handout 3, page 47).

Flipchart or whiteboard to record points during the debrief.

Video camera, tripod, recorder and TV monitor (if required).

LEARNING POINTS AND SKILLS PRACTISED

- All the general interview skills including questioning, listening and the observation of non-verbal signals.
- Planning initial approaches with the other person's motivation in mind.
- The exploration of attitudes and gaining commitment to the plan.
- Influencing skills. The selling of benefits and willingness to bargain to achieve central objectives.

© David Turner 1992, published by Kogan Page

Procedure See notes on the conduct of role plays (Checklist, page 49). Issue handouts to participants and brief them. Allow up to 25 minutes for preparation. Meanwhile brief the observers and set the room up to represent the senior manager's office. Allow play to continue for up to 25 minutes and then give a few moments for players to come out of role before starting the review.

Review See notes on feedback and review in Chapter 2 (Handouts 1 & 2, pages 45 and 46).

In particular, the group should try to answer the following questions as part of the review.

- How well did the middle manager play to his boss's known preferences?
- Did the senior manager understand the benefits he was being sold?
- Was the middle manager prepared to alter his proposals to enhance his chances of being accepted?
- Did the middle manager answer objections and reservations effectively? Had he anticipated possible objections?
- Who did most of the talking? Did the senior manager listen and question well?

HANDOUT
Selling ideas to the boss

Brief for the middle manager

You run a large clerical department in the organization. The operation is very largely computerized although some operations are still manual. The offices, in which your 200-plus staff work, are modern and you have only occupied them for the last 6 months. Unfortunately, the furniture and equipment that you have was moved from your old premises and is pretty scruffy. You have a good team of people, but you are inclined to think that their efforts and their commitment to the company and the job are affected by what appears to be a lack of care and concern for them and their welfare by the company. Neighbouring companies appear to have moved in with everything brand new.

You have costed out what you believe to be essential new equipment (ergonomically designed chairs and workplaces for each computer terminal, rewiring the terminals to a 'ring main' that doesn't trail all over the place, a range of changes to the lighting, new blinds to reduce glare and a few cosmetic/decor items). The total cost is £145,000. You have all the competitive quotations and the ones you have chosen are cheapest by far, with payment over 3 years if required. You have a great deal of information about the benefits of ergonomically designed equipment and of the beneficial effects of improved layouts and lighting.

You are about to see your boss. You want to get his support for your ideas before he takes the plan to the board who will have to make the final decision. You understand that there is about £250,000 of this year's capital budget so far uncommitted. The cost of your proposals is equivalent to about 5 per cent of the wages bill for your department for the year. The improvement in staff morale and the feeling that the company has their interests at heart should produce a real productivity improvement in the order of around 2 per cent. In wages terms that is about £40,000. This could involve a staff saving or the absorbtion of extra volumes in the future at no extra cost.

There are other benefits that are less easy to cost. The principal among these is the health and safety aspect. Improved lighting and reduced glare should lessen the risk of accidents and damage to eyesight. Improved seating and workplaces should improve posture and thus reduce fatigue and possible long term injury potential. As a tentative estimate, from these factors alone, you anticipate a saving of some £15,000 per year in sick pay and temps wages and further productivity increases as well. On this basis it should be possible to construct a case that the expenditure could be recouped in 2 to 3 years. This fits well with the board's directives about payback periods. You know that your boss is a stickler for the rules. Therefore, the payback calculations must be acceptable.

His views on staff welfare and the benefits of looking after staff well are less well known. He is, however, a reasonably receptive person and he is sympathetic to new ideas. But he will need convincing. You are due to see him in a few minutes.

HANDOUT
Selling ideas to the boss

Brief for the senior manager

One of your managers runs the clerical operation for the company with a staff of some 200. They occupy some excellent offices in a new building. The company leased these offices 6 months ago and moved in very quickly to minimize the disruption. In the process you brought all your old equipment with you and so the offices, inside, do not look all that smart. However, the staff turnover is low and you believe that the productivity you achieve is pretty good. There have been no complaints since the move into the new offices and everyone you speak to seems reasonably content. The manager of this clerical operation has told you that she has some ideas for investment that, if accepted, will improve morale and productivity.

You are quite open to ideas, and there is some money (about £200,000 uncommitted so far) available within your budget. You expect another £75,000 to be committed shortly to some new computer equipment for another of your departments.

Every decision about investment over £25,000 has to be agreed by the board, so any new ideas must be readily saleable. Their main preoccupation at present is with productivity and their competitiveness in a very tight recruitment market. They wish the company to be seen as a good place to work. None the less, a good financial case will need to be made too.

You are a great believer in the theory that if you treat your staff right they will respond and work well. You believe in making working conditions and the social side of work as pleasant as possible. However, good equipment and effective leadership are more important, in your opinion, than fancy decor, potted plants and comfortable chairs. People are here to work after all.

The manager, who is due to see you shortly, is a very personable sort of woman. She is everybody's friend and has difficulty when there are hard decisions to be made about people. She has, however, made a good job of the move into the new offices and the operation is proceeding as smoothly as before. Her staff seem to respond well to her and the record of sickness, absence and leaving in her department is as good as any other department's.

PERSUADING A DOUBTER

Role Play 36

Time guide Up to 1½ hours, including 30 minutes for preparation and 30 minutes for debrief.

Participants 2 plus observers.

Equipment Desk, chairs and tables. (Trainers may wish to provide a choice of formal or informal seating for participants to choose their own preferred setting).

Copies of the individual briefs for players of the 2 managers. Copies of both briefs for the observers.

Notes for role players (Handout 4, page 48) if required. Observers' checklists (for an example see Handout 3, page 47).

Flipchart or whiteboard to record points during the debrief.

Video camera, tripod, recorder and TV monitor (if required).

LEARNING POINTS AND SKILLS PRACTISED

- All the general interview skills including questioning, listening and the observation of non-verbal signals.
- The exploration of attitudes, clarification and understanding of objections.
- Planning initial approaches with the other person's motivation in mind.
- Selling benefits and advantages to overcome objections.
- Aspects of the management of change.

Procedure See notes on the conduct of role plays (Checklist, page 49). Issue handouts to participants and brief them. Allow up to 30 minutes for preparation. Meanwhile brief the observers and set the room up to represent the personnel manager's office. Allow play to continue for up to 30 minutes and then give a few moments for players to come out of role before starting the review.

Review See notes on feedback and review in Chapter 2 (Handouts 1 & 2, pages 45 and 46).

In particular, the group should try to answer the following questions as part of the review.

- How sensitively did the personnel manager handle the situation?
- Did the doubting regional manager understand the benefits?
- Was the doubter convinced?
- Was there a commitment to support the proposal?
- Did the proposer take account of the doubter's objections?
- Did the need for a means to sell change to staff feature as a selling point for the committee?

HANDOUT
Persuading a doubter

Brief for the personnel manager

You are the personnel manager of a company employing some 800 people in 16 different premises. One of your objectives, agreed at your last appraisal, is that during the course of this year you will establish some form of consultative forum for management and the workforce to discuss matters of relevance to both. There is currently no structure for consulting staff.

You have researched thoroughly what other organizations do, and have talked to regional managers as well as a large number of staff, and you have devised a scheme. You are very keen that the Staff Committee, as it is to be called, is seen as useful and can address matters of some substance. You are aware that it could, without care, become very trivial and time-consuming – useful only as a safety valve for petty complaints.

Your scheme is as follows: there will be 1 elected member from the staff at each of the 16 offices. There will be 4 managers, 1 from each of the regions, selected on a rolling basis from among regional and area managers. In addition you will act as the secretary and either the MD or the personnel director will chair each meeting.

You have 3 objectives in creating this committee. First, you wish staff to feel that they have a visible influence on things that are done. Second, you wish to enhance the way the company communicates with its staff. Questions can be raised formally about issues that concern staff and managers will have to present information for the attention or consideration of the committee. A much more open system should result. Third, this committee will act as a good sounding board for all the changes that are scheduled for the next couple of years. Long-term warnings of impending change can be given, objections or fears heard and allayed, and alterations to plans made, if necessary, in the light of staff reactions, well before the event.

It is important that consultation is serious. Feedback from the committee must be heard before the proposals are implemented. The areas that you foresee for this type of consultation are discipline, working hours and conditions, inter-department communication, standardizing procedures and practices between areas, ways of overcoming staffing problems (recruitment, absence, etc) and enhancing social and working relationships. This should give the committee some weight and credibility. You also want the committee to consider ways of increasing staff's identification with the company as a whole.

One regional manager, who is on the same grade as you, has expressed to you his strong doubts about the scheme. He is worried, he says, about who will end up managing. He has also seen works committees before and all they end up doing is 'talking tea and toilets'. He doesn't want to waste his time with it. It is important to you to persuade him to support the scheme. You have arranged to meet him in a few minutes.

HANDOUT
Persuading a doubter

Brief for the regional manager

You are a regional manager of a company employing about 800 people in 16 different locations. You have 4 area managers, each responsible for one of the locations reporting to you.

The personnel manager, from head office, spoke to you a few weeks ago about some stupid scheme that was being cooked up to get representatives from all the sites to meet with a load of managers, on a regular basis, as a consultative committee.

The personnel manager (the same grade as you) sees it as a way of involving people in the business, whatever that means, and of giving them a say in what goes on. You and the management team manage the business; what staff can contribute, that they don't already do, you don't know. Apart from which, there are a whole range of changes that are essential and which are about to be made over the next year or so. You don't want these changes upset by some staff committee; the changes are too important.

In your last company there was a works committee. It was a real waste of time and effort. Not only were the topics at issue trivial in the extreme ('tea and toilets' as you like to describe it) but also the time it took, the level of benefit that anyone got from it and its low credibility among staff made it counter-productive. The only people that were elected to it were those with some sort of axe to grind, or with a grudge and determined to score points off the company. You spent many miserable hours with the thing and you do not wish to be dragged into anything like that again. Neither do you want your managers and staff to waste their time on it.

The personnel manager has asked to see you about it and the meeting is due to start in a few minutes. You said what you thought when it was first raised and you will go on saying it.

MISTAKES HAVE BEEN MADE
Role Play 37

Time guide Up to 1 hour, including 20 minutes for preparation and 20 minutes for debrief.

Participants 2 plus observers.

Equipment Desk, chairs and tables. (Trainers may wish to provide a choice of formal or informal seating for participants to choose their own preferred setting.)

Copies of the general brief for both players. Copies of the individual briefs for players of the 2 managers. Copies of all the handouts for the observers.

Notes for role players (Handout 4, page 48) if required. Observers' checklists (for an example see Handout 3, page 47).

Flipchart or whiteboard to record points during the debrief.

Video camera, tripod, recorder and TV monitor (if required).

LEARNING POINTS AND SKILLS PRACTISED

- All the general interview skills including questioning, listening and the observation of non-verbal signals.
- The avoidance of ineffective offensive/defensive behaviour.
- Assessing ways of cooperating in the future.
- Resolving differences constructively.

Procedure See notes on the conduct of role plays (Checklist, page 49). Issue handouts to participants and brief them. Allow up to 20 minutes for preparation. Meanwhile brief the observers and set the room up to represent the operations manager's office. Allow play to continue for up to 20 minutes and then give a few moments for players to come out of role before starting the review.

Review See notes on feedback and review in Chapter 2 (Handouts 1 & 2, pages 45 and 46).

In particular, the group should try to answer the following questions as part of the review.

- How constructively did the managers handle the situation?
- Did the outcome improve the current situation?
- How well did the managers explore what was required for the future?
- Was an attitude of conflict or competition apparent? Was this a row or a problem-solving meeting?
- Was the word 'fault' used? Is this appropriate?

HANDOUT
Mistakes have been made

General brief for all

Accessimport Ltd is a small company importing, marketing and distributing high quality bathroom and kitchen accessories. The goods are manufactured under contract from several different suppliers. They are imported in bulk to reduce freight charges and are assembled (some items are made from parts manufactured separately), packed to order and despatched from your premises.

Output is comparatively steady, there being no major seasonality about the business. The flow of goods in from contractors, the provision of the necessary materials to complete assembly and the packaging materials are the responsibility of the purchasing department. It consists of a purchasing manager and 2 other buyers. This department monitors usage and, in conjunction with your sales staff, forecasts future demand. They have occasionally purchased a little too much stock but this is the agreed policy, given the diversity of origin of some of the components. There is the need for a safety stock to offset any temporary transport, customs or other difficulties.

The operations department handles, stores, assembles, packages and despatches the goods to order. There is an operations staff of 30 people including the manager. They are responsible for the receipt and storage of both products and product parts and of packaging materials for use in despatching the assembled goods.

HANDOUT
Mistakes have been made

Brief for the operations manager

You are the operations manager for Accessimport Ltd and have been in the job for 2 years. You have, in that time, established some effective usage and supply monitoring systems and have reduced the costs of units despatched by some 12 per cent. You have a very steady workflow normally and, given the absence of seasonality, you rarely have problems of supply of either products or packaging and you are able to plan labour requirements and production schedules very closely. It is this that has enabled you to reduce costs; you are very pleased with this achievement.

You rely on the purchasing department for ensuring adequate stock levels. You work quite closely monitoring usage and planned demand for items. Lead times for purchasing on some items, imported from overseas, are quite long so it pays to get it right. They have generally done a good job.

This last week, however, has been a trying one. In fact you cannot remember a worse one. There was a large initial order for a big new customer. This was good news and you laid on overtime and extra transport to cope. Other orders were also at an unusually high level. Last Friday, you checked your stock levels of the necessary packaging items and almost all were satisfactory. You checked the position of the 2 that looked marginal and you were assured that there was a delivery due during the coming week. Fortunately, you were told, both items of packaging came from the same domestic supplier.

During production a new batch of boxes for one of the lines was opened and discovered to be oversize, so that the inner packing and the article inside, a bathroom light and shaver socket, rattled about loose. When you checked, the whole batch, some 3000 cartons, were faulty. You asked if they could be sent back and replaced, only to discover that this batch came from a supplier now in liquidation and further supplies had not yet been negotiated. You had to use bubble pack as a space filler. This had to be acquired, which wasted time. Work in progress had to be moved aside and stored while you waited for bubble pack to arrive.

Worse still, the promised delivery of the marginal items failed to arrive. Everything else from that supplier arrived but not the two items you needed. Fortunately, your stock of one item held out but you were several thousand short on the other. This item, a sticker illustrating the correct method of wiring electrical appliances must, by law, be enclosed with each appliance despatched. It turns out that the last delivery was much smaller than it should have been, by some thousands, and no one had discovered it. Half way through the run you sent for more and discovered there were none, despite the stock records figures kept by your department. More delay, confusion and cost, and customers not receiving what was promised. You estimate an unnecessary cost of some £3000 has been incurred in labour, materials and transport. You have to account for this and you blame the purchasing manager, who has failed to provide what you need when you need it. You are going to see her shortly.

HANDOUT
Mistakes have been made

Brief for the purchasing manager

You have been the purchasing manager of Accessimport for several years and you are very proud of the job you have done.

For the first time in a long time, last week saw some problems. You know that the operations manager is very unhappy about some of the mistakes. He came to see you 2 weeks ago and checked with you on the supply and availability of the materials that he needed for what looked like being a heavier than usual week. He was anxious about 2 lines, both of which, according to the delivery schedule produced from your purchase orders, were due to be delivered during last week. In addition the stock records kept by the operations department showed that there was just sufficient stock already available in store. There should have been no problem as the supplier for both is local and is generally reliable. The delivery of these 2 items did not materialize and it appears that one of your buyers had transposed the date on the delivery schedule.

With one line it was not a problem but then you discovered that all the stock records for the electrical wiring instructions were wrong. Everything stopped on the affected lines for 2 days while new supplies were sought. This sticker has to be included with electrical articles by law. The only explanation you can come up with is that the last delivery was a long way short of the advised figure. The stores failed to notice the discrepancy and so it is their fault that they are now short. They took them in and reported the delivery to you and the invoice was duly paid. You will have to go back and try to get credit for the shortage, which will be difficult this long after the event. They need to improve their checking procedures.

The worst problem was the boxes for the light/shaver sockets. For some reason the last delivery that was brought out for use during the week had been of boxes of the wrong size. The whole batch of 3000 printed cartons was too big. You had to rush around and get bubble pack to allow the operations people to continue packing the line. They were shouting at you for the 2 days it took you to negotiate a good price. Worse still, the original supplier of the boxes has now gone into liquidation and you can get no redress. No new supplier has yet been found. You could be criticized for failing to see the trouble coming with that supplier. You have spent half the weekend trying to fathom out what happened and discovered at last that in placing the order, which you had done yourself, you switched the printing specification with another similar but larger box on the purchase order. This means that the other line, with which you switched it, is also wrongly sized (too small). You checked a sample and it is. No one else knows that yet.

You are on your way to talk to the operations manager. You will want to sort out the checking procedures and explain away some of your department's (and your own) errors.

MID-CAREER CRISIS
Role Play 38

Time guide Up to 1 hour, including 20 minutes for preparation and 20 minutes for debrief.

Participants 2 plus observers.

Equipment Desk, chairs and tables. (Trainers may wish to provide a choice of formal or informal seating for participants to choose their own preferred setting.)

Copies of the individual briefs for players of the manager and employee. Copies of both the handouts for the observers.

Notes for role players (Handout 4, page 48) if required. Observers' checklists (for an example see Handout 3, page 47).

Flipchart or whiteboard to record points during the debrief.

Video camera, tripod, recorder and TV monitor (if required).

LEARNING POINTS AND SKILLS PRACTISED

- All the general interview skills including questioning, listening and the observation of non-verbal signals.
- Mirroring and summarizing as ways of crystallizing thoughts and attitudes.
- Encouraging self assessment, self appraisal and reflection to shift the decision-making back to the employee.
- Not making reassuring promises that cannot be kept.

Procedure See notes on the conduct of role plays (Checklist, page 49). Issue handouts to participants and brief them. Allow up to 20 minutes for preparation. Meanwhile brief the observers and set the room up to represent the manager's office. Allow play to continue for up to 20 minutes and then give a few moments for players to come out of role before starting the review.

NB. It should be possible to use the structures and career paths within the group members' organizations as the basis for discussions. Players can identify clearly with those – only limited detail is given here in the briefs.

Review See notes on feedback and review in Chapter 2 (Handouts 1 & 2, pages 45 and 46).

In particular, the group should try to answer the following questions as part of the review.

- Did the interview help to clarify the employee's thinking?
- How well did the manager explore what was required for the future in the employee's situation?
- How well did the manager listen and encourage self analysis?
- Were the possibilities open to the employee, and the means of achieving them, explored?

HANDOUT
Mid-career crisis

Brief for the manager

You are a senior manager in the organization and one of the sections that comes under your control is the work study section. This small group is employed throughout the organization on a range of routine tasks and also on some projects involving work study, method study and measuring skills. Your level of day-to-day control of their work is very limited but you are their senior line manager.

The section manager is a long-serving, loyal and conscientious employee who is due to retire in 2 or 3 years. He is a product of the section and has only limited management skills. He has, however, coped reasonably well, allocating his resources to where they are required. This job has been made easier by the generally self-motivated, quiet and analytical type of staff in the section.

One of the section's staff has asked to see you for some 'advice on his career'. You do not know this man very well but you have seen him at work and talked to him occasionally. Following his request for an interview, you spoke to the section manager to get an assessment of his performance and potential.

It appears, from his manager's comments and from your own observations, that this man is a bit introverted but is a very competent member of the team. He was promoted a couple of years ago and is now one of the 2 senior members of the section below the manager. He has been involved in some quite complex method studies lately and done well with them. The client departments certainly seem pleased with the outcomes of those projects.

His skills are technical ones. He does not inspire confidence from his manner, and his ability to relate to other people and communicate, except on paper, is low. If there were a down side to this man's performance it would be in the area of communication skills. He has upset a few people around the place by trying to impose ideas and failing to listen to or take account of others' objections.

From what you can see there are not many places for this employee to go, except perhaps as the successor to the current section manager when he retires. Even then he would have to improve his way of dealing with people.

HANDOUT
Mid-career crisis

Brief for the employee

You have been working in the work study section for a long time. Your duties are fairly mundane as the section's task is to maintain working methods, to measure performance and to evaluate new machinery and methods in the business's offices and production facilities. All this is done with the standard work study techniques which you have been using for 15 years. For the last 2 years, since your promotion to a more senior grade, there has been an improvement. You now become involved in more complex and interesting problems. The design of new layouts and paperwork systems are areas in which you feel you have done quite well. The routine work of measuring and monitoring still goes on.

You have worked for the current section head for some time. You get on fine but he has little to do with you except to allocate the jobs that need to be done. He is a nice enough old chap and he has managed to keep the section together and reasonably busy and well regarded through the organization.

However, over the last few months you have become increasingly restless and dissatisfied. You are not sure what you want to do. Ever since you left college 20 years ago, you have been involved in work study in one form or another. You have become very skilled and the use of those skills to solve problems and set up new practices and procedures has always been, until now, something of a challenge. You like working on your own, problem solving. People tend to get in the way and raise objections to the methods emerging from your work. It is a pity that they cannot always see the benefits. You find it frustrating that they seem unwilling to accept your ideas straight away.

It strikes you that you ought to be trying for a position of more responsibility. You would welcome the extra money that a management job would mean and you feel that, with your detailed knowledge and understanding of the way this business works, you might be valuable as a manager somewhere. You are certain that you could devise and run a very efficient system and use your skills to make continuous improvements to it. Given the position, you would be able to impose efficient and effective systems much quicker.

You do not know how to go about it and you are still not sure that that is what you really want anyway. Your appraisals have always been sound and as far as you know you are reasonably well regarded. You need to explore what is possible and whether there really are openings elsewhere in the organization for you. You want something different, something more than stopwatches, graphs and flow charts. Maybe it's a fish farm!

You have asked to see the departmental manager, under whose overall control your section comes, for some advice about your career.

THE THORN IN THE FLESH

Role Play 39

Time guide Up to 1 hour, including 20 minutes for preparation and 20 minutes for debrief.

Participants 2 plus observers.

Equipment Desk, chairs and tables. (Trainers may wish to provide a choice of formal or informal seating for participants to choose their own preferred setting.)

Copies of the individual briefs for players of the 2 managers. Copies of both the handouts for the observers.

Notes for role players (Handout 4, page 48) if required. Observers' checklists (for an example see Handout 3, page 47).

Flipchart or whiteboard to record points during the debrief.

Video camera, tripod, recorder and TV monitor (if required).

LEARNING POINTS AND SKILLS PRACTISED

- All the general interview skills including questioning, listening and the observation of non-verbal signals.
- Mirroring, reflecting and summarizing as ways of crystallizing thoughts and attitudes.
- Encouraging self assessment, self appraisal and reflection and gaining acceptance of a need to improve.
- Establishing goals and objectives for improvements in behaviour.

Procedure See notes on the conduct of role plays (Checklist, page 49). Issue handouts to participants and brief them. Allow up to 20 minutes for preparation. Meanwhile brief the observers and set the room up to represent the senior manager's office. Allow play to continue for up to 20 minutes and then give a few moments for players to come out of role before starting the review.

Review See notes on feedback and review in Chapter 2 (Handouts 1 & 2, pages 45 and 46).

In particular, the group should try to answer the following questions as part of the review.

- Did the interview clarify the problem to the administration manager? Did he accept that it was his behaviour and attitude that created problems?
- Did the managers explore what was required for the future?
- How well did the senior manager listen and encourage self analysis?
- Were the possibilities open to the employee, and the means of achieving them, explored?
- What else can the boss do to improve the situation?

HANDOUT
The thorn in the flesh

Brief for the senior manager

You have been the manager at this site for 3 years and you have, as your assistant, a middle-aged manager whose main task is the control of the administration function. This includes budgeting and management reporting, invoicing, costing, building maintenance and wages. There is an office staff of 7 people to assist with these tasks.

The administration manager has a logical and intelligent mind. He is a devout Christian, with a great love for his family and he expresses concern for the welfare of all your staff. He is well educated, to degree level, and has a good understanding of management theory and of the needs of your particular business. In fact he has a very full grasp of the major issues at any time and is able very quickly and succinctly to reach to the root of problems. He is quite creative with ideas for improvement to the operation and is more often right in his predictions than he is wrong. The day-to-day administration of the site goes very smoothly and with the absolute minimum of problems. But, despite all these qualities, he is a thorn in your flesh.

He is aware that his intelligence and analytical skills are superior to those of the rest of the team. This, and his tendency to be right, are not sold short. Everyone is aware when he is right again. He loses no opportunity to criticize the actions of others in the team if mistakes are made and will make complaints freely to you if there are disagreements between him and other managers. On these occasions he adopts a whining tone as if to try and prevent possible criticism of his own performance. Despite his ability to see solutions he seems incapable, or at least very unconfident, in putting things into action. When he does try to pursue some plan of his own, or of yours, he usually manages to upset someone or to lose his temper or to come running to you to complain that so and so is being difficult.

He expresses himself clearly and is not reluctant, in private or at meetings, to voice his criticisms of what is happening at the time. Challenge him and he will become stubborn and surly. He resents direct criticism himself. He seems to feel insecure in his position and this is shown by the speed with which he will blame others and run to you for help and support. His manner is often abrasive and he gets little cooperation from other managers or the staff. This creates a vicious circle of complaint and criticism. In his dealings with you he is either whining or a little ingratiating even though he is constantly presenting you with suggestions for action. When you have agreed to some of these and given him the task to do, the usual round of criticisms and complaints has started up again.

Other managers are beginning to voice their views about him to you. The time has come to try to address the problem. This manager's behaviour is affecting the performance of the whole team.

HANDOUT
The thorn in the flesh

Brief for the administration manager

You have been the administration manager on this site for about 3 years. Your boss is the site manager and you are responsible, among other things, for budgeting and management reporting, invoicing, costing, building maintenance and wages. There is an office staff of 7 people to assist with these tasks. You run a tight ship and things seem to run pretty smoothly.

You are 45 years old and are devoted to your family. You have a degree and a lively analytical mind. You are a Christian and are concerned for the good of people everywhere. You try to show that Christian concern at work. The other managers in the team are a somewhat sorry lot. They are not a particularly bright bunch and seem to spend a great deal of their time in misdirected and totally wasted activity. You have tried to point out the less effective things that are going on, both to your boss and to other members of the team, but they seem unwilling to accept that you are right. So much so that when you do try to put things right or improve things they become uncooperative and obstructive. You have complained to the boss about this repeatedly, but she seems to do nothing.

All this is beginning to tell on you. You are beginning to lose confidence and you are concerned lest your own performance shall be called into question. It is increasingly difficult to remain calm amid all the mistakes and criticisms that are flying around. Why can't they see that you have a point? Why won't they accept that you are right sometimes? If only your boss would listen – you try hard enough to please her. You have never criticized her, you have always accepted her judgements. Ideas that you have put up she has developed, and then she has turned round and got you to try and implement them. This has put you in the position of having to try to sell the ideas to the rest of the management team, who are not keen to listen or cooperate. You have virtually decided to pull back and concentrate solely on the day-to-day running of your section. The trouble with that is that you rely very heavily on the others in the management team for information and for cooperation in seeing the procedures through. You are considering throwing it all up and looking elsewhere for a job. It seems to you that either some of the other managers or you will have to go.

THE RESENTED PROMOTION
Role Play 40

Time guide Up to 1 hour, including 20 minutes for preparation and 20 minutes for debrief.

Participants 2 plus observers.

Equipment Desk, chairs and tables. (Trainers may wish to provide a choice of formal or informal seating for participants to choose their own preferred setting.)

Copies of the individual briefs for players of the supervisor and the storeman. Copies of both the handouts for the observers.

Notes for role players (Handout 4, page 48) if required. Observers' checklists (for an example see Handout 3, page 47).

Flipchart or whiteboard to record points during the debrief.

Video camera, tripod, recorder and TV monitor (if required).

LEARNING POINTS AND SKILLS PRACTISED

- All the general interview skills including questioning, listening and the observation of non-verbal signals.
- Dealing with conflict and emotion.
- Assertiveness and controlling conversations.
- Encouraging reflection and an acceptance of the nature of the problem.

Procedure See notes on conducting role plays (Checklist, page 49). Issue handouts to participants and brief them. Allow up to 20 minutes for preparation. Meanwhile brief the observers and set the room up to represent the supervisor's office. Allow play to continue for up to 20 minutes and then give a few moments for players to come out of role before starting the review.

Review See notes on feedback and review in Chapter 2 (Handouts 1 & 2, pages 45 and 46).

In particular, the group should try to answer the following questions as part of the review.

- Did the interview clarify the problem to the storeman? Did he accept that it was his behaviour and attitude that created problems?
- How well did the supervisor explore the causes of the problem?
- Did the storeman accept the need for the situation to change?
- What else could the supervisor do to improve the situation?
- What would the effect be on the rest of the group?

HANDOUT
The resented promotion

Brief for the supervisor

Three weeks ago you were promoted to be the supervisor of the stores team to which you have belonged for the last 4 years. Previously you were one of 2 senior storemen. You worked hard for the promotion and are very pleased with it. You get on well with the boss and with most of the team.

You have one problem team member and he is the remaining senior storeman. He is likely to be quite busy since he is now left with all the tasks you used to do together. These include the handling of cash from customers and the replenishment of stock from suppliers up to an authorized limit.

You and he were quite friendly. You would occasionally go for a drink after work, your children go to the same school and play together at each other's houses and your wives meet from time to time to go shopping or whatever.

Since your promotion it has become very difficult. He is reluctant to accept your instructions, however pleasantly put. He is surly and uncommunicative and has begun to try and turn the rest of the team against you. Several times you have glimpsed him talking to one of the team, sniggering and gesturing or looking in your direction. A couple of times the conversation has dried up in an embarrassed kind of way when you appeared. On the day your appointment was announced and you went to talk to him about how you might work together, he turned on his heel and walked away. He hasn't really spoken to you since.

You intended to assist the man with the senior's duties, once you have got a better understanding of your own specific tasks, since there appears to be no one who is immediately promotable to fill the post left vacant by your promotion. Now there seems to be a real bridge-building job to be done. Your wife, who has spoken to his a couple of times since your promotion, has had no indication that there is any resentment in the family as a whole and she can see no reason for it. You can think of no occasion on which you might have upset him. It is becoming a problem and the rest of team are being affected by it. The time has come to find out what his problem is and to get back to some semblance of normality.

HANDOUT
The resented promotion

Brief for the storeman

You have worked here for 6 years as a senior storeman. Three weeks ago the other senior storeman was promoted to be the supervisor of this stores group; so he is now your boss. You resent this quite deeply. The more you think about it the more it rankles.

Not only are you now going to have to do, on your own, all the tasks you used to do together but you also realize that there is no one to promote to help you. These tasks include the handling of cash from customers and the replenishment of stock from suppliers up to an authorized limit. But the worst thing is that you can't understand why he was promoted and you were not. You have been here longer than he has (by 2 years) and you do a perfectly good job.

You and he were quite friendly. You would occasionally go for a drink after work, your children go to the same school and play together at each other's houses and your wives meet from time to time to go shopping or whatever. The friendship is now over as far as you are concerned, though your wife has said she intends to go on seeing your new supervisor's family and cannot understand why you are so upset about his good fortune.

Now that he's in charge you have recognized just how much you wanted that job. You are going to see that he fails. If you are uncooperative and if you turn the rest of the team against him he will find it very hard to succeed and may decide to quit. In any case if he does mess it up he won't last long. So you are not helping him at all and you have started telling the other team members embarrassing stories about him (the mistakes he made when he first arrived, the telling off he had from the boss over a row with a customer – that sort of thing).

He has asked to speak to you at the end of the day today but you are not going to be all buddy buddy with him now – let him sink!

Chapter 9:

Five-minute role plays for face-to-face communication skills

This chapter has a slightly different purpose from the preceding chapters. The short role play scenarios here all relate to everyday occurrences at work and provide the opportunity for people to practise their communication skills. Elements of the skills that can be practised in the longer role plays in earlier chapters will be present here as will all the very basic inter-personal skills.

These scenarios can, of course, be used as a resource from which to choose relevant examples in just the same way one would from the others in this book. However, they can also be used to great effect as the first in a series of role plays, as a taster, to remove some of the anxieties associated with 'play acting', and to accustom trainees to this type of activity.

The sort of skills that can be practised with these 'quickie' role plays include:

- assertiveness;
- listening;
- questioning;
- understanding body language;
- influencing;

- giving feedback and constructive criticism;
- basic coaching techniques;
- handling conflict;
- controlling conversations.

In addition, they can be brought out at very short notice, with the absolute minimum of preparation by the tutor or trainer, when a situation arises in session that could be improved by the role play approach. Introduced with some remarks such as '. . . Yes, I like that approach you describe. Let's see how it might work. I have a situation here . . .' one of these short role plays can serve to illustrate, confirm and enliven the lessons being learnt (and, maybe, to stimulate some more).

TRAINER'S NOTES FOR ALL FIVE-MINUTE ROLE PLAYS

Time guide Each one of these role plays should only take about 5 minutes to act out. In addition there will need to be a few moments for preparation (up to 5 minutes) and maybe a further 5 minutes for review. Generally, none should take longer than a quarter of an hour from start to finish but occasionally one will generate more discussion and take a little longer in the review.

Participants In most cases there are 2 players (role play no. 60 requires 3). If these role plays are being run in groups of 3 (see below) there will also be an observer. In larger groups there will be more observers, of course.

Equipment Desks or tables and chairs and enough photocopies of the briefs for those involved. The copies of the notes for role players (Handout 4, page 48) and checklists for observers (see Handout 3, page 47) can be issued if required but are not essential.

If these role plays are being used to familiarize people with the activity on video then they provide an excellent opportunity to try out the video equipment and accustom the group to seeing themselves on the screen.

LEARNING POINTS AND SKILLS PRACTISED

These short role plays allow for most of the basic lessons in communication skills to emerge. These include:

- interviewing techniques of questioning and listening;
- observing non-verbal signals;
- summarizing;
- influencing;
- controlling conversations.

Procedure There are 3 possible procedures beyond the standard one described in Chapter 2 (Checklist, page 49). They are:

1. The familiarization exercise.
2. The use of triads or small groups.
3. The spontaneous opportunity.

1. The familiarization exercise

- Explain the concept of role playing and describe the procedure.
- Introduce the first one as a trial and use some of the anxiety reducing techniques from Chapter 2.
- Issue briefs and explain the role of the remainder of the group as observers while the participants prepare. Bring the participants together and start the play. Be prepared to stop and restart if nerves, giggles or embarrassment get in the way. Pass off the interruptions as natural at first.
- Review the exercise, talking the group through it. If video is being used, play it back first and maybe play important bits later if the experience of seeing themselves has been too distracting.
- Reiterate the purpose of role playing, play down the embarrassment and the interruptions, emphasize the successes and congratulate all involved.

2. The use of triads or small groups (see Chapter 3)

- Explain the concept and the procedure. For each role play 2 people will play the roles and the third will act as the observer and will lead the discussion after the play. The group then rotates roles until all the chosen scenarios have been played out.
- The principal points at issue should be spelt out at the start and everyone instructed to take particular notice of these.
- Split the group into threes (triads) or other convenient groups and separate them. This does not have to be in separate syndicate rooms as it can be managed quite easily around the training room.
- The trainer should visit groups in turn, listening to the conversa-

tions, helping with the feedback, and answering questions on the way round.

- Once all the groups have finished, or the time available has expired, call the groups together and run a plenary review. Discuss in particular those issues highlighted at the start.

3. *The spontaneous opportunity* (see Chapter 3)

- Prior to the session, if the learning points are such that a role play may be appropriate but not pre-planned into the programme, select 1 or 2 appropriate scenarios from this chapter. The trainer can keep these in reserve for use when necessary.
- When an occasion arises in which the learning would be enhanced by a role play, introduce one as a chance to try out the approach in practice.
- Proceed as for any role play either with 2 participants and the remainder as observers, or as described above for triads.
- After the play is finished, draw out the lessons learnt from the observers or from the small groups. If this is the first time the group has come across role playing, the trainer will need to lead the review carefully to ensure the points are covered.

Review In all 3 cases the review should be a similar process. Notes on feedback and review are in Chapter 2 (Handouts 1 & 2, pages 45 and 46).

Among others the group should try to answer the following questions:

- How well did the players discover the facts? How effective were the questions?
- Did they approach the interview with an open mind? How well did they listen?
- Did both parties feel that they had achieved what they wanted?
- How effective was the approach that they chose? Were the problems sensitively addressed?
- Could the outcome have been different with a different approach?

THE LUNCHTIME CELEBRATIONS

Role Play 41

HANDOUT

Brief for the office manager

You are the sales office manager and you have recently promoted to section leader a young man who has impressed you with his enthusiasm and effort. Hard-working and popular, he seemed the ideal candidate, with plenty of potential. Today he arranged for a few of his colleagues to join him for a lunchtime celebration of his promotion. Alcohol during working hours is strictly forbidden by company rules. The lunch hour is from 1.00 to 2.00 pm and at 2.15 you went to talk to the new section leader but he was not there. Twenty minutes later you tried again only to find him in the middle of an uproar, with the office and him reeking of whisky. You asked him to come and explain why the office was in chaos, why the alcohol, and why he was late back from lunch. Why on earth he should blot his copybook in the first few days of his new job you cannot imagine – have you made a mistake promoting him?

THE LUNCHTIME CELEBRATIONS

Role Play 41

HANDOUT

Brief for the section leader

You have just been promoted to section leader in the sales office. You arranged today for a group of your colleagues to join you for lunch to celebrate your promotion. Your lunch hour is from 1.00 to 2.00 pm but because of a bomb scare on the route back to the office you were 30 minutes late back, something you don't think your boss is aware of. You are well aware of the company's rule about no alcohol during working hours so none of you drank anything at all except mineral water during your meal. As you came back into your section office it was immediately clear that 3 of your staff were the worse for drink after they had been out to celebrate the birth of a child. They, too, had come back late from lunch, moments before you, and were causing a great deal of disruption in the office. You tried to sort it out, calm things down and get the office back to work but one of the lads managed to spill a plastic cup containing whisky all over you and your desk. At that moment your boss arrived, took one look and told you to come into the office. You are not too bothered as you can explain the fracas quite easily.

THE EARLY FINISHER
Role Play 42

HANDOUT

Brief for the manager

In your section in the factory you have noticed that one of your employees now regularly stops work at his bench a good 15 minutes early and starts clearing up. The standard practice is that staff stop 5 minutes before time and tidy up and brush down machinery, etc. Lately, since this one member of staff has started doing it, others have also taken to stopping a bit early, but none quite so blatantly. This situation cannot continue and you now wish to take him to task over it.

THE EARLY FINISHER
Role Play 42

HANDOUT

Brief for the employee

You started work here several years ago when you lived just down the road. Now your family has grown you have had to move away to find a bigger house. Prices were such that you have had to move some distance and the only bus you can get at the end of the day leaves very shortly after finishing time. If you miss it you have to wait another hour for the next one. So to ensure a speedy getaway you've taken to stopping a bit early to ensure you are first out and away to catch this bus. You are pretty sure the boss has noticed and he's asked to see you.

WHY CAN'T HE WORK OVERTIME?

Role Play 43

HANDOUT

Brief for the manager

You run a vehicle repair workshop for a large agricultural contractor. During certain periods of the year there is the need for everyone to work a great deal of overtime at weekends. One of your team, who has particular skills with hydraulics, is asked to work almost every weekend. He is very reliable and has hitherto been content to turn out at weekends.

Today is Thursday and the coming weekend is a Bank Holiday and, as it is the height of the harvest season, it is critical he is there to see to any breakdowns. This morning you put the call out for overtime this weekend as usual but your foreman tells you that this particular member of staff is not prepared to work it.

This could cause you some real problems so you have asked to see him to get him to work at least part of the weekend.

WHY CAN'T HE WORK OVERTIME?

Role Play 43

HANDOUT

Brief for the employee

You work in the vehicle repair workshop of a large agricultural contractor. You like the job and because of the nature of the work there are times when a lot of overtime is available. You like this and work about as much as you can get. It helps to pay the new mortgage you've taken out but your wife has been complaining recently about the amount of time you are working and you have decided to take this weekend, a Bank Holiday, off to take the family to the seaside. It is all booked, hotel and everything, and the whole family is really excited about it. It will be the first complete weekend that you will have had off for 10 weeks. In fact, now that you think about it, you have only had 3 or 4 days off in nearly 3 months. No wonder your wife is complaining.

This morning the usual call for people to work the weekend came round and you have let it be known that you will not be available. You haven't spoken to the manager about it but you know that your not being available will be a problem for him. Still, it's too late for that now and he'll have to lump it. He has now called for you to go and see him.

THWARTED AMBITION
Role Play 44

HANDOUT

Brief for the manager

In the course of your regular discussions with all your members of staff you recently talked about promotion prospects with one young member of your team. He is very keen and ambitious and even though he only joined you about 6 months ago, you spent some time reviewing various possibilities, including the fact that there was likely to be a vacancy for an assistant manager very shortly. You made no promises, nor do you think you left him feeling as if he had a good chance of the job. It came up as an example of the type of thing you might consider him for at some unspecified date in the future.

The vacancy has arisen and you have filled it from elsewhere in the organization with someone more experienced than your man. It is due to be announced shortly. Your team member has now asked to see you and your secretary tells you that he is pretty upset about the appointment which seems to have leaked out. He is a promising young chap and just because he hasn't got this one does not mean his career is blighted.

THWARTED AMBITION

Role Play 44

HANDOUT

Brief for the employee

You have been with the organization for about 6 months. In a recent chat with your boss he led you to believe that he had you in mind for promotion and a forthcoming vacancy for assistant manager could be yours when it arose. He also said he had no reason to complain of your performance; in fact he said he was pleased.

In the pub last night one of the secretaries from another department told you that the job had been filled by one of the people in her section. You were amazed. You now feel totally let down. Why didn't he tell you? Is it too late, if it hasn't been announced yet? What's wrong with you? You thought the job would be yours. Goodness knows when the next opportunity will occur.

You have asked to see your boss to thrash this out.

THE LATE REPORT
Role Play 45

HANDOUT

Brief for the department manager

Two months ago you asked one of your assistant managers for a report describing the information needs of the department. This was to be the first step in the process of enhancing the computer systems. You wanted a clear picture of what information was used, where it came from and how reliable it was. You also wanted the information classified by its use (ie each job in the department was to be listed with its information needs). The deadline was today and your assistant manager has sent you a note to say that he hasn't finished it and that it should be ready in about a fortnight. This annoys you since only 2 weeks ago you asked if there were any problems and were told there were none.

Your brief is to produce an overview of the department's whole requirement for computer systems in the next 5 years. Your boss is due to speak to you next week and you are only waiting for this report to finish yours. You did emphasize its importance when you asked for it. You have asked your assistant manager to see you.

THE LATE REPORT

Role Play 45

HANDOUT

Brief for the assistant manager

Two months ago your boss gave you a project to do. It was to record the information requirements of the department in terms of its use, sources and reliability. She said it was to contribute to something she was doing for her boss on the computerization needs of the department for the future. It was due to be finished today. It isn't. You have found it extremely boring, and the help you have had from others in the department has been minimal. They don't seem to be interested. In any case, every job you have examined (you have now looked at them all) seems to have a very wide range of sources of information which the people who perform them assume you know about or forget to mention. This is, presumably, because they are so familiar with it themselves it has become second nature. Because of this it has taken you weeks to gather the information in the detail in which it was required.

You now have to write the report. You sent your boss a note to say you will have it ready in a fortnight. The only thing you are bothered about is that you found the task so boring that you failed to tell her about your difficulties or to ask for help – even when she asked.

THE TEMPORARY TRANSFER

Role Play 46

HANDOUT

Brief for the supervisor

You have a group of 7 people working for you in your section and all are very busy on their own clerical tasks. Your manager has told you to assign, for a week, one of your staff to the neighbouring section, which is snowed under with work. You argued that you were pretty busy too and could not afford to lose anyone, but you were overruled and convinced that you had to help.

Two of your people used to work there and could, therefore, make a difference straight away. You know one of them is away for 2 days later this week for a distant funeral so that leaves you with a choice of one. You know that he is heavily involved in a project that he is doing, as part of his job, towards his qualification exams and that it is due to be finished next week. In fact you have been advising him on it and you know how much work there is left to do. Nevertheless, you have to tell him to leave it, during work hours anyway, to go and help the other section next door.

THE TEMPORARY TRANSFER

Role Play 46

HANDOUT

Brief for the office worker

You are working in a section of 7 people doing a range of clerical jobs. You are very busy at present with your normal workload and a project that you have from the department manager. This project is to do with the work of your section and needs to be done, mostly anyway, in working hours. The section has been very busy for some time and there is a lot of this project left to do. It is due in next week and will count in a big way to your passing, you hope, the next stage of your professional qualification. You could be put back by 6 months if you miss it. Your supervisor has been helping you with it.

It is very interesting work and you think you can get it done if you spend a fair bit of time on it at work this week and at the weekend to finish off writing it up. Your supervisor has just asked you to pop in to the office when you've finished what you are doing.

THE SCRUFFY SALESMAN
Role Play 47

HANDOUT

Brief for the sales manager

You run a team of 10 sales staff covering a large slice of the country. You have been remarkably successful as a team selling to the financial services sector.

One of your team, although he meets all his targets, is worrying you. He is scruffy and unkempt and his car is a mess. A couple of customers have remarked to you that he always looks as if he's slept in his clothes. He doesn't seem to recognize the importance of appearance, particularly in your market where formal and smart working dress is customary.

Another customer has complained, unofficially, about a row that this man had with their buyer. It appears that he became quite aggressive and almost rude. It is only a small firm but you do not want to upset and lose them. You wish to remind this man of the need to retain good relations with all his customers.

You have asked him to come and speak to you.

THE SCRUFFY SALESMAN

Role Play 47

HANDOUT

Brief for the salesman

You are a salesman selling to the financial services sector. You have met all your targets recently and have built up a good rapport with your customers. You have a quality range of products and will defend them to anyone.

A couple of days ago a buyer of a small customer criticized one of your products and the resulting discussion became a bit heated when he wouldn't accept what you were telling him. But you believe he was wrong and you defended the product vigorously.

Your sales manager has asked to see you and you suspect it is about the argument. You still think you were justified in shouting. In the past year, your boss has had a go at you about your appearance too.

OLD HAND –
NEW MANAGER

Role Play 48

HANDOUT

Brief for the department manager

You have been newly appointed to the department as the manager. You have come from another organization in the same trade but you know very little of your new employer other than what your new director has told you. You are 30 years old and this appointment is a big step up for you. The boss tells you that he is expecting you to get to grips with the department, shake it up and get it to be much more responsive, flexible and forward thinking.

Your third day here you have set aside to speak to those people that report to you. You were introduced on the day you arrived but have not yet had a chance to talk to them properly. You are now keen to get to know them and to start to establish a rapport.

You have taken no advice from others about your people, preferring to make up your own mind. The personnel manager, when you met her yesterday, did say you might have a problem with one supervisor who had been around a long time but she didn't have a chance to say why. That supervisor is due to see you in a few minutes.

OLD HAND – NEW MANAGER

Role Play 48

HANDOUT

Brief for the long-serving supervisor

You are 52 years old and have worked your way up to where you are today by sheer hard work over the last 20 years. You started on the bottom of the ladder and you are proud of what you have achieved. You believe in running a tight ship and you don't want the efficient and friendly nature of the work and your relations with staff to be upset. You have a nice quiet set up and you want it to continue.

The director told all the supervisors a few weeks ago that a new manager for the department had been appointed, but when you were introduced a couple of days ago you were dismayed to discover this person is a young whiz-kid from one of the firm's competitors. You foresee all sorts of change for change sake, 'new brooms' and trendy theories.

The new person is seeing all the supervisors in the department today and you are next in. You want to make it plain that you run a good operation and want no interference. You want to be left alone to get on with it. There have been no complaints so far and that's the way you want it to continue.

THE COMMITTEE MEMBER

Role Play 49

HANDOUT

Brief for the committee chairman

You chair the management committee of a small local voluntary organization. Your committee meets regularly every other Thursday evening. One member of the committee rarely appears at meetings but bombards you and the committee with objections to whatever you propose. There are a lot of new things you want to do for fund raising and to further the work you are doing and this one committee member stands in the way of almost everything that is put forward.

He is a very busy man and provides a great deal of money for your cause as well as providing many of the facilities that you use on his company's premises. Therefore you cannot afford to lose his support. He was also a former chairman, and he and his influential cronies used to provide the bulk of your funding. Most of them have now retired, died or moved away and you need to change the image of the organization to appeal for support to a wider public. You do need him to agree to some of the committee's suggestions in order to make progress and you have arranged to meet him shortly.

THE COMMITTEE MEMBER

Role Play 49

HANDOUT

Brief for the committee member

You have been a member of this voluntary committee for many years and until about 5 years ago you were the chairman. You do not have a great deal of time to attend meetings but you are very conscientious in giving your views about proposals being put forward.

Just lately some of the ideas that are coming forward have been preposterous. You would never have agreed to putting them forward when you were chairman. You provide a great deal of support for the committee in cash and facilities from your company. You enjoy doing this and it enhances your standing in the community.

When you were chairman you organized a network of leading citizens to fund and support the work of this group. They actually provided the bulk of the funding for the organization and, of course, it raised their profiles locally (and why not?). It has been very successful, even if some of them are now retiring and becoming less influential. You want this network to continue.

The current chairman has asked to see you.

CAN HE TAKE A HOLIDAY?

Role Play 50

HANDOUT

Brief for the marketing executive

You work in a very busy marketing department. Besides the 6 product managers, there are two other executives employed like yourself to handle national publicity, shows and exhibitions. Your next show is the major national trade show in late August and the arrangements are well in hand.

These last few months have been hectic, although very successful for you personally. You have therefore arranged to take a fortnight's holiday with your family. You are going to be away from it all in the Dordogne. You will be away from Friday 17th June until Monday 4th July. It is now 1st June, your holiday is booked and you are due to pay the balance of the cost this week. Because you booked late a big deposit has already been paid. You checked with the office holiday planner, your dates clash with nobody and you also cleared it with your boss last week.

You are really looking forward to it and feel you need the holiday. Your boss has asked to see you shortly.

CAN HE TAKE A HOLIDAY?

Role Play 50

HANDOUT

Brief for the marketing manager

You run the marketing department for your company. Apart from the 6 product managers there are 3 national promotions executives. They have all been very busy for the last few months, so much so that one of them is currently off sick suffering, according to his doctor, from nervous exhaustion. You have just been told by the board to make sure that there is a company presence at the International Fair in Tokyo. It is to take place in mid-July. A stand has been booked. This is not something that was in the original programme or catered for in the budget. You have extra funds and, now, very little time to prepare for it. Your product managers are committed, one promotions executive is off sick and the second is getting married on 2nd July and then going on honeymoon. The only person available is the other promotions executive – and he has booked a holiday for the last 2 weeks in June.

It is now 1st June and time is at a premium. You must ask him to put off his holiday until after Tokyo. You propose to assist him in the preparations for this show and the stakes are high. This show has a very high profile. He is on his way to see you.

PRAISE AND DEVELOP
Role Play 51

HANDOUT

Brief for the manager

You are the manager of a development department whose task it is to plan, organize and control layout and equipment changes in the manufacturing division of the company. One of your staff, a graduate aged 24, has just completed a project to install a new layout of conveyors, sorters and packing machines at the end of a line producing small plastic bottles. This has been highly successful, the manager of the line and the staff working on it are all pleased with it and prefer it to the original layout.

Now is the time to talk to your young graduate, show how pleased you are with this project and its conclusion and try and discover which areas are ones in which further help, training and development of skills are required.

PRAISE AND DEVELOP

Role Play 51

HANDOUT

Brief for the graduate

You have been working for 1 year in this development department whose task it is to plan, organize and control layout and equipment changes in the manufacturing division of the company. You have just completed a project to install a new layout of conveyors, sorters and packing machines at the end of a line producing small plastic bottles. This has been highly successful, the manager of the line and the staff working on it are all pleased with it and prefer it to the original.

Your boss has asked to see you. You hope he is as pleased as you are with the outcome of this project. If you get the chance you would like to become involved in an automation and computerization project next. You have heard that the main line producing the shrink-wrapped 6-pack of half-litre bottles is due to be automated further later this year. You would like to do that. The most difficult issue during this last project was negotiating with several different companies for the purchase of the conveyor equipment; their salesmen were fairly aggressive and you found it difficult to deal with them.

THE TRANSFER
Role Play 52

HANDOUT

Brief for the employee

You have been working here for the last 3 years and your appraisals have always been above average. Your manager has never had cause to take issue with you about any of your work so you are fairly sure that you are well regarded. You know the systems here very well and you handle one or two prestige customers on a personal basis.

You have seen an internal advertisement for the job of assistant manager in the next-door department. You would like to apply for it, since there appears to be no chance of promotion in this department. You know the work of the next-door department backwards since you worked there before taking your present job and you have been loaned to them on several occasions recently when they were busy.

You have asked to see your boss 'on a personal matter' and you want an endorsement to your application.

THE TRANSFER

Role Play 52

HANDOUT

Brief for the manager

One of your staff has asked to see you on 'a personal matter'. You have arranged a meeting in a few minutes. This member of staff is invaluable to you. Your computer system in the office is fairly complex and you employ many temps, who frequently have problems with it. This staff member can sort out all these problems as well as being the main source of detailed knowledge of the systems. In addition you have a private customer, the old Duke of Whitehall, who spends a great deal of money with you and will only deal with this one person. This is historical and stems from the day you upset him over a complaint and this member of staff resolved it shortly after, to the Duke's great satisfaction.

You have this person in mind for promotion but there are no vacancies in the foreseeable future. There is a need for some basic 'people skills' training but otherwise this person is well qualified for promotion. It is nearly time for the annual appraisal and you were going to discuss this then.

You hope that nothing serious is wrong; you'll just have to wait and see what is said when you meet shortly.

THE WANDERING MAINTENANCE MAN

Role Play 53

HANDOUT

Brief for the site manager

You are the manager of a small subsidiary site a few miles from the main factory building of the company you work for. You have a staff of about 100 and the plant and machinery that you use is maintained by the factory maintenance staff. One of that team is assigned primarily to you. He is a very hard man to find. He is constantly moving between the sites, is on call to the factory as well as to you, and he drives a company van.

You are certain that he is playing you off against the maintenance manager in the factory and that his actual productive work is minimal. If he is not with you he claims to have been in the factory and vice versa. If you start checking he has always been out collecting materials or parts. His manager is less worried. He values the man's skills for the occasions where an urgent repair is needed and you must admit that when it is important he can work wonders with the equipment. You want to keep tabs on him and to establish more control over him and his use of time (after all, your budget is charged for him). You have arranged to see his manager about him or arrange for a different fitter to be allocated to you.

THE WANDERING MAINTENANCE MAN

Role Play 53

HANDOUT

Brief for the maintenance manager

You manage a team of 12 maintenance workers. All of them, with one exception, normally work in the factory where you are. They have different trades but they are all capable of doing most of the jobs required to maintain the plant and machinery on site. Only occasionally is it essential to have a particular tradesman for a difficult task. One of the team is assigned to work at a detached site a few miles down the road. He is one of your most capable men and has a very sound knowledge of all the company's equipment and of that at the detached site in particular. He has been known to work near miracles with broken down equipment. He does have to come back to the factory to use the workshop, speak to you and to borrow tools etc. He has the almost permanent use of a fitter's van to ease the moving between sites. The manager of the detached site has been complaining that he doesn't have any control over this 'resource' of his and wants to talk to you.

This man is one of your team, he does not come under the site manager, and you are in control of his work. You decide what are his priorities and you are not going to pass control to anyone else.

ALLOCATING AN UNPOPULAR JOB

Role Play 54

HANDOUT

Brief for the supervisor

You are responsible for a section in the offices of a manufacturer of wheels, castors and specialized hinges. Every year the company takes a stand at the trade show and each year a few people from the offices are needed to help set up and take down the stand. The people involved end up having to run around all over the place at the beck and call of each and every salesman. The work involves fetching and cleaning stock, moving it around, packing and unpacking it, loading, unloading; it's a long list.

This year your section has been detailed to provide 1 person. It has always been an unpopular job – hard work with no appreciation – and you have to find someone to do it. Your choice is one of your staff who has not done it before (there are others who have not either). You chose this person for their usual cheerfulness and general willingness and because you felt there would not be too many objections. You must emphasize the need for the job to be done and done properly. It will involve travel and a couple of nights away.

ALLOCATING AN UNPOPULAR JOB

Role Play 54

HANDOUT

Brief for the office worker

You work in the offices of a manufacturer of wheels, castors and specialized hinges. Every year there is a trade show and a few people are nominated to go and help set up and take down the stand that the company has there. This job is very unpopular because those chosen work extremely hard at unfamiliar and dirty tasks for which they get nothing but impatience from the salesman and more running around to do. While the sales staff supervise and do all the talking, it is the office staff who rush about, get filthy, work long hours and get no perks at all. It seems that there is no overtime paid and all you get is some free sandwiches at midday and your overnight accommodation (in a cheaper hotel than the sales staff). Those who have done it seem to think that they were treated badly while they were doing it. You have never had to do this job before but you have heard all about it. You know that your section has to provide somebody this year, you overheard the manager talking about it and you do not want to do it. You do not want to be away from home and the job strikes you as a really horrid one. Somebody else can do it. Your supervisor has just asked you to come and see her in a few minutes and you think she'll ask you to do this show job.

PERSONAL HYGIENE
Role Play 55

HANDOUT

Brief for the supervisor

You work in a large office and you have 25 staff working for you. One of your staff is causing you and the rest of the team a problem. He is very smelly. At times on hot days the smell of stale sweat becomes overpowering. There are other signs of a lack of personal care – dirty fingernails, a dirty neck and permanently greasy hair.

Your staff have tried heavy hints and nothing seems to sink in. They have now raised it as a formal complaint to you and you have arranged to see this smelly member of staff to try to remedy the situation.

PERSONAL HYGIENE

Role Play 55

HANDOUT

Brief for the employee

You work in a large office with some 20 or so other people. You keep yourself very much to yourself and find the rest of the group a bit rude and not very friendly. They have made quite a lot of rude remarks about 'body odour' and so on which you find upsetting.

You are aware that you have been unable to keep yourself as clean as you would like recently, since you have moved into a caravan which is not connected to all the main services, but you do try. You have been there for the last 4 months since your marriage broke up and your finances took a real beating. Your job here is not well paid and the maintenance you pay, plus the repayments on the debts you and your ex-wife accumulated, take everything you have. There is no immediate prospect of things improving for quite some time.

Your supervisor has asked to see you – you do not know what for, but it is almost certainly not a raise!

THE COFFEE CIRCLE
Role Play 56

HANDOUT

Brief for the site manager

You are the senior manager of a small detached site. You have 4 other managers working for you and there are 2 secretaries. Your offices are all together at one end of the general office in which the small administration staff work. None of you, managers or secretaries, are tied to a particular start and finish time and it has become a custom for you all to arrive at roughly the same time and share a cup of coffee and a gossip for a few minutes before starting the day. This you find a very easy and effective way of keeping the team together and picking up the issues of concern to the various sections. It only takes a few minutes and is a nice sociable thing to do, which in no way detracts from the effectiveness of the people concerned.

The administration manager is coming over for a chat.

THE COFFEE CIRCLE
Role Play 56

HANDOUT

Brief for the administration manager

You work in a small detached site and are in charge of the administration and the administrative staff of 8. Your office is at one end of the section and the other managers and their 2 secretaries have a group of offices at the other end. Over the last few weeks, this group, including the site manager who is your boss, have taken to gathering for a few minutes at the start of each day over a coffee for a general chat. This is all very cosy and you would like to join the circle. No one in the group, or you, are bound by start and finish times but your staff are. You try quite hard to ensure that your staff arrive on time and start work promptly. This has increasingly become a problem when your team can see and hear very clearly everything that is going on at the other end of the office. They resent the fact that they have to get straight down to it while this group of bosses has time to gossip. You want your manager to do something about it and have asked to talk to him.

THE AFFAIR AT WORK

Role Play 57

HANDOUT

Brief for the manager

You are the manager of a small factory. This weekend you have left work behind and have decided to catch up on your gardening.

At work one of the cleaners is having an affair with one of the fitters. Both are married and it is public knowledge at work that this is going on. Because their work is different, there is no problem as far as you are concerned as their manager. It is after all, literally, their affair. You were pondering this, while planting your potatoes, when a leather-jacketed and helmeted figure appears at the bottom of your garden.

THE AFFAIR AT WORK

Role Play 57

HANDOUT

Brief for the cleaner's husband

Your wife works as a cleaner in the local factory. She has been doing so for several years. Just lately she has been behaving strangely to you and her hours at work have become irregular. You suspect her of having an affair. This lunchtime in the pub (today is Saturday) you were talking to one of the people who works with your wife who let slip that she was seeing a lot of the fitter at work. Your wife's boss lives just down the road – you'll go and ask him. So you climb on to your motorcycle and dash round there. You are angry and confused. As you remove your helmet at the bottom of the boss's garden he comes across to talk to you, to find out what you want.

CONFLICTING INTERESTS

Role Play 58

HANDOUT

Brief for the workshop manager

You are the workshop manager for an articulated trailer hire company. Your trailers must be inspected and tested by the Department of Transport at regular intervals. One trailer, T345, is due for inspection in a week's time and the appointment has been made with the testing centre. It normally takes a fitter 2 or 3 days to prepare a trailer for the test. You notified the contracts manager in writing, a week ago, of the inspection date, of when you need the vehicle and that you would arrange collection and delivery of a replacement trailer. Today you have despatched one of your fitters with a tractor unit to collect the trailer from the customer's yard taking another trailer with him. The fitter has just rung in to say that the trailer is loaded for a journey and will not be available for 4 days. This means that you will have to make the journey again, pay a couple of fitters to work over the coming holiday and reschedule your workload – again. Either that or cancel the inspection date, lose the fee and wait until after the current test certificate has expired to get the trailer through. It will not then be available for hire. You are going to sort it out with the contracts manager.

CONFLICTING INTERESTS

Role Play 58

HANDOUT

Brief for the contracts manager

You are in charge of renting articulated trailers. One of your best customers has just rung up to say that a driver has arrived with a trailer to replace T345 which he has on hire, which has to go for a Department of Transport test. This is the first that he had heard of it and it is now too late because it is loaded and just about to leave on a 3-day journey. It will be back at the end of the week, just before the holiday weekend. He says you can have the trailer then. You told him that was fine and to send the driver back.

Normally the workshop produces the testing programme, notifies you of specific dates and arranges collection of the trailer, replacing it as they do so. All your people have to do is notify the customer and ensure that the trailer is free for collection. It has worked quite well, but you would like more control over when trailers are and are not available. You don't know what happened this time but the workshop manager does have a habit of trying to lay down the law. It is time you tried to take a bit more control.

SEEKING OPINION

Role Play 59

HANDOUT

Brief for the senior manager

You run a large department with several different sections. A supervisor in one of the sections has applied for the vacancy of section manager in another. After interview you have almost decided to give her the job. She appears conscientious, intelligent, willing and ambitious. Her annual appraisal reports have all been good and you consider that she could do the job very well. Before offering the job you wish to obtain the opinion of this woman's current section manager about her performance and, in particular, her performance as a supervisor.

SEEKING OPINION

Role Play 59

HANDOUT

Brief for the section manager

One of your supervisors has applied for a vacant section manager's job. If she got it you would be on equal grades. You have watched this young woman creep her way up the ladder. You do not like her; it is difficult to put a finger on it but you don't trust her. Her work appears excellent, mistakes are few and her team seem to work well for her. There has never been any friction that you know of but you just find she annoys you. She seems to try to ingratiate herself with anyone in a senior position and it seems to work; she has done very well in the short time she has been with the organization. Before you know it she could be your boss! That would be terrible for you. She is always polite to you and after the first few days she hasn't tried the sycophantic act on you. Your boss has asked you to go and speak about this young woman. You couldn't stand it if he were about to offer her the job.

CUSTOMER COMPLAINT

Role Play 60

Please note there are 3 handouts to this role play. It will need to be played in two parts: (1) Customer and employee and (2) Customer, employee and manager. The manager intervenes at the point that seems most appropriate to the trainer.

HANDOUT

Brief for the customer

You have been a regular customer of this motor service and parts organization for a long time. You know the manager of the parts department very well. You are responsible for a large fleet of company cars. A recent invoice for the supply of parts is wrong and you have come down personally with the intention of getting it altered. You want it altered straight away and you do not want any messing about. This is the third invoice in a row that has been wrong so you want prompt action from somebody and you will go to the top if necessary. You are very annoyed. A young assistant is behind the counter.

© David Turner 1992, published by Kogan Page

CUSTOMER COMPLAINT

Role Play 60

This role play will need to be played in two parts: (1) Customer and employee and (2) Customer, employee and manager. The manager intervenes at the point that seems most appropriate to the trainer.

HANDOUT

Brief for the assistant

You are 20 years old and have worked for this motor service and parts company for a year. You are standing behind the counter of the parts department with a monumental hangover after a party last night and you were late in this morning, so you are bound to be told off by the manager.

A man in a suit has just walked in looking angry and you are not keen to deal with him. If you can you will get rid of him. You cannot take any aggravation this morning - you do feel ill! The man comes up to speak to you.

CUSTOMER COMPLAINT

Role Play 60

This role play will need to be played in two parts: (1) Customer and employee and (2) Customer, employee and manager. The manager intervenes at the point that seems most appropriate to the trainer.

HANDOUT

Brief for the shop manager

You work in a busy motor parts store and you have 3 store/sales staff working for you. One of your staff is only 20 and thinks he knows everything. He was late in this morning and you intended to have a word with him. You were just about to call him in when you hear raised voices outside your office. It sounds like this young chap being very rude to a customer. From the voice you recognize one of your most valued customers. You know him very well. You go to sort it out.